IMPROVING SUSTAINABILITY IN THE HOSPITALITY INDUSTRY

Over the past few years the hospitality industry has become a lot more sustainable than it used to be. However, the industry's contribution to the sustainable development of our societies is still significantly smaller than it could be. This book specifically addresses the links between operations, tactics and strategy from a sustainable development perspective and moves beyond describing *what is* to reflect on *what could be* or even *what should be*, thus providing students with a concise guide for improving sustainability concepts and businesses in the hospitality industry.

Each chapter uses specific cases and examples to reflect on different ways in which sustainability principles can be used for revisiting the host–guest relationship and improving the industry's business processes and models. In doing so, the book provides current and future professionals with guidelines, inspiration and a call for action to take sustainability within the hospitality industry to the next level, based on inclusiveness, equality and a sustainable relationship with our natural environment.

Frans Melissen is a Professor of Sustainable Business Models/Sustainable Experience Design at the Academy of Hotel Management of the Breda University of Applied Sciences, the Netherlands.

Lieke Sauer is a Lecturer of Sustainable Business Models at the Academy of Hotel Management of the Breda University of Applied Sciences, the Netherlands.

Hospitality Essentials Series
Series Editor: **Roy C. Wood**, Faculty of Business and Law, University of Northampton

Hotel Accommodation Management
Edited by Roy C. Wood

Strategic Questions in Food and Beverage Management
Roy C. Wood

Improving Sustainability in the Hospitality Industry
Frans Melissen and Lieke Sauer

For more information about this series, please visit: www.routledge.com/Hospitality-Essentials-Series/book-series/RHE

IMPROVING SUSTAINABILITY IN THE HOSPITALITY INDUSTRY

Frans Melissen and Lieke Sauer

Routledge
Taylor & Francis Group

LONDON AND NEW YORK

First published 2019
by Routledge
2 Park Square, Milton Park, Abingdon, Oxon OX14 4RN

and by Routledge
711 Third Avenue, New York, NY 10017

Routledge is an imprint of the Taylor & Francis Group, an informa business

British Library Cataloguing-in-Publication Data
A catalogue record for this book is available from the British Library

Library of Congress Cataloging-in-Publication Data
Names: Melissen, Frans, author. | Sauer, Lieke, author.
Title: Improving sustainability in the hospitality industry / Frans
Melissen and Lieke Sauer.
Description: Abingdon, Oxon ; New York, NY : Routledge, 2019. |
Series: Hospitality essentials series | Includes bibliographical references
and index.
Identifiers: LCCN 2018025637 (print) | LCCN 2018042210 (ebook) |
ISBN 9781315164755 (Master ebook) | ISBN 9781351675093 (Web
PDF) | ISBN 9781351675079 (ePUB) | ISBN 9781351675062
(Mobipocket) | ISBN 9781138057692 (hbk : alk. paper) | ISBN
9781138057708 (pbk : alk. paper) | ISBN 9781315164755 (ebk)
Subjects: LCSH: Hospitality industry--Management. | Hospitality
industry--Environmental aspects. | Social responsibility of business. |
Sustainable tourism. | Sustainable development.
Classification: LCC TX911.3.M27 (ebook) | LCC TX911.3.M27 M45
2019 (print) | DDC 647.94068--dc23
LC record available at https://lccn.loc.gov/2018025637

ISBN: 978-1-138-05769-2 (hbk)
ISBN: 978-1-138-05770-8 (pbk)
ISBN: 978-1-315-16475-5 (ebk)

Typeset in Garamond
by Integra Software Services Pvt. Ltd.

For all those who want to contribute to making our world more hospitable for all

Contents

Figures

Case studies

Acknowledgements

First, we would like to express our gratitude to Emma Travis and Carlotta Fanton at Taylor & Francis/Routledge for their support for this book and their guidance during the preparation. We would also like to thank Xavier Font, Nadia Teunissen, Hans Westerbeek, Lars Moratis, Yoy Bergs, Helene van Straten, Bert Smit, Joseph Roevens, Rob van Ginneken, Jasper Bosma, Tim Brown, Geoff Marée, Stan Josephi and Jörn Fricke, for providing us with tips and inspiration for cases, and Gienke Osinga, Simen Kooi and Anne van Delft, for giving us the time and freedom to embark on our plan to write not just another sustainability book about *what is*. We also thank all of our colleagues at Breda University of Applied Sciences for their understanding and allowing us to put in the time needed to focus on *what should be*.

Finally, we would like to thank the Hospitality Essentials series editor and our friend, Roy Wood, for encouraging us to take on this challenge.

Frans Melissen and Lieke Sauer
Breda
May 2018

Introduction

As indicated by its title, this book focuses on sustainability in the hospitality industry. It is not the first book to do so. In fact, a number of textbooks, but also edited works and (popular) science books, all addressing this topic in some way or another have been published over the years. Many of them are dedicated to describing best practices and case studies related to implementing or using specific (more) sustainable technologies, processes or materials in hospitality settings. Others provide current and future hospitality professionals with inspiration and explanations with respect to specific cutting-edge approaches to particular aspects of sustainability within particular contexts. Some focus on the applicability of particular sustainability concepts, such as cradle-to-cradle or the circular economy, in the hospitality industry and either elevate one of those concepts to a panacea or explain in detail why the peculiarities of this industry make it especially difficult or even impossible to apply it. Whereas some of these books address the link between day-to-day operations in hospitality businesses and sustainability, others look into the relevance of sustainability for decision-making at the strategic level.

Therefore, you might ask why we would need another book on this topic. The honest answer is that we, the authors, feel we could add something to the collection of resources already available to you, the reader, that seems to be missing: A perspective on how to take sustainability in the hospitality industry to a next level. Numerous initiatives and programmes dedicated to introducing (more) sustainable practices have certainly made this industry more sustainable than it used to be. A lot of progress has already been made. However, this has not (yet) resulted in a true integration of sustainability into the business models, strategies, tactics and day-to-day operations applied by the vast majority of hospitality businesses and professionals. The hospitality industry is not yet fully aligned with the concept of sustainability. It is not yet making the contribution to sustainable development of our societies that it could make. This book explains why and, more importantly, explores avenues to change this situation. Therefore, it goes beyond addressing the most obvious links between operations, tactics, strategies and business models in hospitality on the one hand and sustainable development on the other. Instead of describing *what is*, this book explicitly focuses on *what could be* or even *what should be*.

The rationale for this book

A number of other books have already looked into the details of particular technologies, processes and certification schemes that could reduce the environmental impact of, for instance, hotels and restaurants. We would never claim that we could do a better job of describing the details of those technologies and processes than the writers of those books. In fact, this book will not even attempt to provide you with a full overview of best practices or (the details of) certification schemes relevant to the hospitality industry. Instead, it focuses on the concept that this industry lends its name to: hospitality.

In other words, this book does not tell you how to install LED lighting or water-saving showerheads, nor the associated returns on investment. What it does do is look into the relationship between hosts and guests in hospitality settings, and how this relationship impacts people's behaviour, also in relation to possible energy-saving or water-saving technologies and measures. The reason for doing so is that sustainable development cannot be realised only through technological advancements; it requires new behavioural patterns of people. Those patterns will not emerge from nowhere but need to be purposely stimulated and cultivated, based on a thorough understanding of what people need, want and desire.

The rationale for this book is that the hospitality industry could fulfil a crucial role in stimulating and cultivating sustainable behavioural patterns of a number of people. Not only guests, but also employees, local residents of the neighbourhood in which a hospitality establishment is located, other businesses and professionals, policy-makers, and so on. From a sustainable development perspective, the (potential) impact of successfully fulfilling this role is likely to significantly outweigh the direct impact of measures such as installing energy-saving or water-saving technologies.

This is not to say that such measures should not be taken. Of course they should and we encourage you to make full use of all checklists, guidelines, examples, tips and tricks already available to help you to do so. However, in this book we argue that this is not enough to truly integrate sustainability into hospitality concepts and businesses. This is also not enough for the hospitality industry to achieve its full potential with respect to furthering sustainable development of our societies.

Therefore, this book explicitly focuses on what would be needed to realise this potential. It reflects on avenues to move from treating sustainability as an add-on to business as usual to using sustainable development principles as a powerful concept and guideline for revisiting the host–guest relationship and improving the industry's business processes and models.

Set-up and style

Consequently, the set-up of this book is a little bit different from most textbooks (on hospitality and sustainability). Even though it consists of separate chapters, like most other textbooks, these chapters are actually parts, or building blocks, of an overall storyline. You will not find separate chapters on the people, planet and profit aspects of sustainable development, nor chapters dedicated to particular sustainability problems, such as water, biodiversity, climate change or poverty. Instead, each chapter provides a part of the argumentation of what could probably best be described as a call for action. This call for action explains how the hospitality industry could realise its full potential regarding its contribution to sustainable development of our societies.

This call for action kicks off with an exploration of the relationship between the hospitality industry and sustainable development of our societies. It then moves on to establishing the key role of behaviour in pursuing sustainable development, also – and maybe even especially so – in the hospitality industry. Subsequently, promising avenues for stimulating (more) sustainable decisions and behaviour of people are explored and explained. The next steps in this call for action show that successfully following these avenues needs to be based on creating a match between your identity, as a hospitality provider, and the way you engage in sustainability initiatives, as well as establishing a sustainable relationship between your business and the local community and (local) natural environment. Once these building blocks are in place, hospitality businesses and professionals could focus on new ways of organising hospitality, for instance through joining forces with grassroots movements and collaborating with so-called sharing economy initiatives instead of fighting them. Finally, all of these elements are then combined to create the contours of truly sustainable business models that could be applied in the hospitality industry. This book concludes with describing the key role of current and future hospitality professionals in shaping this sustainable future of the industry *and* our societies, and, obviously, ends with making an appeal to hospitality professionals to take up that challenge.

An overview of the remainder of this book

The remainder of this book comprises six chapters.

Chapter 1 explains the concept of sustainable development and why it represents our biggest and most urgent societal challenge. It then discusses the current situation in the hospitality industry with respect to tackling this challenge. Based on this discussion, this chapter concludes with highlighting why the hospitality industry's contribution to achieving sustainable development of our societies need not be limited to reducing its own (direct) negative impacts. In fact, three reasons are distinguished that explain why this particular industry is actually perfectly positioned to move well beyond this limited perspective on sustainability.

Chapter 2 then links these three reasons to the topics of energy management, waste management, water management, sustainable food and drinks, and the building (materials and furnishing). It further builds on the rationale presented in the first chapter by highlighting why some hospitality businesses and professionals to date find it difficult to apply a progressive approach to dealing with sustainability but also by arguing that some of these barriers are based on overcomplicating matters. Most hospitality companies could do (a lot) more, from a sustainable development perspective, than they currently dare or choose to do. The chapter concludes with explaining that pursuing sustainable development, as a hospitality business or professional, need not always be complicated or involve huge investments. Rather, it represents a choice and requires a focus on people instead of technology.

Chapter 3 explores this crucial role of people in achieving sustainable development in more detail. It highlights the impact of contexts shaped by the hospitality industry on people's decisions and behaviours, and reveals some of the underlying mechanisms. It then moves on to reviewing how these mechanisms both explain the unsustainable course our societies are on and how they could be used to adjust this course, also, and maybe even especially, in the hospitality industry.

Chapter 4 reviews how accounting for the values, preference and priorities of your customers needs to align with the values, intentions and priorities of your hospitality company. It highlights and explains the relevance of aligning your overall identity, as a company, with your identity when it comes to sustainability and the context you create for your customers. If you are to convince your customers to buy and consume the sustainable hospitality experiences you offer them, and support you and get involved in making your sustainability measures and initiatives a success, you need to send a coherent and appealing message through all of your decisions and actions. This chapter concludes with explaining why and how your employees need to be involved in creating and sending that message.

Chapter 5 focuses on the crucial role of local communities, social networks and bottom-up innovation in achieving sustainable development of our societies. If a hospitality company wants to have a maximum positive impact on putting our societies on a more sustainable course, it needs to establish a sustainable relationship with its immediate surroundings, both the (local) natural and social environment. In fact, this chapter explains why tapping into so-called grassroots movements and local (sustainable) developments is a must for any hospitality company, both from a sustainable development and a traditional business-economic perspective.

Chapter 6 then connects the final dots and translates the train of thought presented in all previous chapters into a call for action to hospitality businesses and professionals. It explores the implications of this call for action for the business models that hospitality companies need to create and apply, and it highlights crucial additions to the (traditional) competencies that current and future hospitality professionals need to master to answer to this call.

Hospitality and sustainability

Introduction

To understand the relevance of the hospitality industry for sustainable development of our societies, we first need to understand what sustainable development means. Therefore, the next section addresses the origins and meaning of the terms sustainability and sustainable development. The subsequent sections then provide an exploratory appraisal of the relationship between hospitality and sustainability. As part of this appraisal, we review the current status of addressing sustainability and the way the concept of social responsibility is interpreted and applied in the hospitality industry, the crucial role of reporting, communicating and transparency in all this, and the (perspectives and behaviours of) key stakeholders. Together, these elements set the stage for a preliminary assessment of both the current and potential contribution of the hospitality industry to achieving sustainable development of our societies.

Sustainability and sustainable development

In this day and age, numerous companies use the word 'sustainable' as an adjective to describe their products, services and processes. Many politicians also use it to specify the type of economic growth they pursue through their decision-making. More and more consumers seem to prefer, or at least are willing to try, products and services that are marketed or labelled as 'sustainable'. For some products, processes or decisions, 'green' is considered to represent a synonym for 'sustainable' by many. Green energy is sustainable energy. Greening your home means using more sustainable materials and sustainable, or less, energy. Green growth is economic growth that supports sustainable development of our societies.

Somehow, these particular characteristics of the products and services we, consumers, buy and consume to satisfy our needs have become important to us. In fact, they have become so important to us that some of the companies who provide them feel the need to overstate their case when it comes to the actual environmental (or social) impact of their products, services and processes. In a world in which sustainability apparently has become an important quality, some are tempted to mislead consumers with respect to the actual benefits of what they produce and offer, and the way in which they do so, or at least exaggerate a little. This is usually referred to as 'greenwashing'. In fact, greenwashing has become so common that most consumers nowadays more or less assume some exaggeration to be part of any message by companies, or politicians for that matter, referring to their sustainability performance. Unfortunately, this also means that whereas more and more of us, in our roles as consumers and voters, feel sustainable development is important, quite a few of us have also become rather sceptical regarding the motives of those claiming to be or act sustainable.

This scepticism, which has sometimes even turned into cynicism, is something that clearly needs to be addressed and tackled if we, as humanity, are to achieve sustainable development of our societies. It is a topic we will return to repeatedly in the remaining chapters of this book. However, before doing so, we need to have a full understanding of what 'sustainable' and 'sustainable development' actually mean. What is it that we are aiming for when we say we want to achieve sustainable development? What are the characteristics of products, services and processes that would actually make them contribute to (increasing the chances of us) achieving this objective, and thus make them qualify to be labelled 'sustainable'? The fact of the matter is that answering these questions unequivocally is not that easy.

Even though the origins of the concept of sustainability can be traced back to hundreds of years ago, it would be fair to say that two specific reports have really catalysed widespread discussions about this concept amongst academics, politicians, thought leaders and the business world. The first is entitled *The Limits to Growth*, which was written by the so-called Club of Rome in 1972. Representatives from academia, civil society, diplomacy and industry from around the world founded this *club* in 1968. In their report, they warn that the continued growth of the Earth's population, combined with increased food production, pollution and the (excessive) use of non-renewable energy sources, such as oil, gas and coal, will cause serious problems for all of us. In fact, they use the words 'a rather sudden and uncontrollable decline in [. . .] population' (Meadows *et al.*, 1972, p. 183) to elaborate on the gravity of the situation. They were not the first to warn that the way we, humans, exploit our planet's resources to satisfy our needs could very well lead to us harming or even destroying our surroundings and, ultimately, ourselves. However, what makes this report different from earlier warnings is that it came with some very specific and detailed predictions of what would happen if our behaviour did not change in this respect. What makes this report especially relevant and influential in any discussion on sustainability and sustainable development is that even today, close to five decades after its publication, these predictions pretty much describe exactly what has happened since. In other words, these predictions have so far proven to be ominously accurate.

The second report that is referred to in many discussions on sustainable development is *Our Common Future* by the United Nations' World Commission on Environment and Development (UNWCED), chaired by former Prime Minister of Norway Gro Harlem Brundtland and therefore also known as the

Brundtland Commission. This commission defined sustainable development as 'development that meets the needs of the present without compromising the ability of future generations to meet their own needs' (UNWCED, 1987, Chapter 2, item 1). In essence, this report describes our common challenge, as humanity, to create a world in which the needs of all people can be satisfied in a way that accounts for the limitations in what our planet can provide in terms of resources. In other words, finding a way to satisfy our needs that prevents the predictions of the Club of Rome coming true. As straightforward as this definition may sound, it is important to realise that the Brundtland Commission added some crucial explanations to this definition in their report. For instance, they stated that with respect to the needs of people, it is important to realise that *all* people have 'legitimate aspirations for an improved quality of life' (UNWCED, 1987, Chapter 2, item 4), not just those fortunate enough to live privileged lives or be born in rich parts of our world. This means that meeting the needs of people goes beyond just providing food and safety but also encompasses issues such as education, belonging somewhere and the chance for self-development.

Achieving a state of development of our societies that would qualify as sustainable development is quite a challenge. Especially if you realise that we, as humanity, currently already use more resources than Earth can provide in the long run. If you combine this realisation with the predicted growth of our world's population and the fact that significant portions of the population currently live their lives in circumstances that certainly do not meet the criteria for a decent quality of life, let alone an improved quality of life, the gravity of the situation becomes clear.

Numerous news reports, documentaries, newspaper and magazine articles, blogs and vlogs, personal stories and the like about the current state of both our environmental and social systems further illustrate the gravity of the situation. As a result, most people in our world are now more or less aware of the situation and share a sense of urgency. Most of us realise that our societies are currently on an unsustainable course and measures are necessary. Climate change and poverty, hurricanes and armed conflicts, pollution scandals and a range of health problems all have one thing in common. They could all be argued to represent signals from our planet, combining into one very clear message: you, humans, better change the way you have arranged your world to satisfy your needs, and fast! The fact that these signals have not only continued but have actually become stronger and more worrying over recent years also implies that the way in which we have so far targeted achieving sustainable development is clearly inadequate. The situation cannot be resolved by simply *balancing* the outcomes of individual decisions based on the well-known three pillars of sustainable development: people, planet and profit. This is too slow, leads to sub-optimisation and ignores the ethical and systemic dimensions of the required change. To put it bluntly, simply recycling some materials and turning the thermostats in our houses down a notch will not be enough. We will need to drastically change the way we – consumers/voters, businesses and politicians – make decisions in order to change the distribution of wealth across our globe, how we account for the needs of (different groups of) people, our technological systems, our production systems, and more. We will return to this in more detail in the remaining chapters of this book. First, the remainder of this chapter reviews the current contribution of the hospitality industry to achieving sustainable development of our societies.

CASE 1.1

Sustainable development goals and transparency

Introduction

In 2000, the United Nations (UN) established the Millennium Development Goals (MDGs). These eight goals included targets with a main focus on people and prosperity. Ending hunger, reducing poverty, increasing educa-tion and fewer (victims of) diseases were some of the goals set. In 2016, the Sustainable Development Goals (SDGs) were established, which build on the MDGs. These goals also focus on the Planet aspect and represent a shift in thinking towards addressing sustainable development in general, and as a whole. All 193 members of the UN have signed up to realising these goals. The goals serve as a reference point and guideline for the UN until 2030. All 17 goals interconnect with each; success for one goal affects success for others. The issues discussed affect everyone on the planet and therefore involve all of us to make the world a safer, more prosperous and more sustainable place for all humanity.

Figure 1.1 The 17 Sustainable Development Goals

Source: https://www.un.org/sustainabledevelopment/news/communications-material/

SDGs and the hospitality industry

Ever since all members of the UN undersigned the SDGs, numerous local and global initiatives have emerged for trying to achieve these goals. Some of these initiatives focus solely on the tourism and travel industry, including the hospitality industry. The Impact Travel Alliance (ITA) has set up one of these initiatives. They have organised a series of events in their 30 hubs around the world, bringing three global issues to the forefront. By using these 30 hubs, ITA activates the global community on a local level. The International Tourism Partnership (ITP) is an initiative with the sole aim of connecting the world's large hotel chains, as they believe working together makes you stronger. ITP focuses on the four SDGs addressing water, carbon, human rights and youth unemployment. Another example is from the Pacific Asia Travel Association (PATA), who has announced that they will advocate for increased gender equality in 2018, which is a fundamental human right. This requires investing in education, vocational training and skills development for women, so that they feel empowered to make choices for their future.

Risks and opportunities of applying SDGs for/in the hospitality industry

The SDGs were set on a global scale, thus constituting a clear reference point for partnerships or other initiatives. However, this also means that the SDGs are a political agreement, setting national targets for countries, not companies. Therefore, companies could easily ignore the SDGs and refer to national governments as the ones who bear responsibility. Another risk is that the colourful SDGs are only used to *spice up* Corporate Social Responsibility (CSR) policies and reports rather than actually resulting in actions to achieve the goals because there are no accreditation bodies or measurement policies in place to determine who qualifies for actually assisting in achieving these goals and who does not. In other words, the SDGs are vulnerable to greenwashing. Finally, the way the SDGs have been established and communicated by the UN allows and actually very much invites parties such as individual companies to focus on some SDGs, and ignore others that are equally important, just because they are easier to align with business as usual. Simultaneously, and fortunately, there are examples of companies who have adopted all 17 goals and have chosen a more holistic approach, for instance through joining forces with other companies. Another pro of the SDGs is that they are framed to stimulate innovation rather than being formulated as something you *have to do* based on specific minimum requirements. Goals like Sustainable Consumption and Production could very well actually become the driving force for new business models.

Good or bad example?

Melia Hotels International released a statement in November 2016 that they will incorporate the SDGs in their CSR policy. When looking for evidence on their website, it is not clear where the SDGs tie in (into their overall strategy and day-to-day operations) and how they will be/are being reported on. This raises some doubts about the transparency and genuineness of such a claim. However, Melia still seem to be involved with quite a few interesting sustainability initiatives because they do *pop up* regularly when looking for best practices of CSR in the hospitality industry, for instance on social media or in professional and scientific literature. We will leave it to you to decide whether this is the result of clever communication and good marketing or a genuine desire to do good and acting upon that.

Source: United Nations, http://www.undp.org.

Melia Hotels, https://www.meliahotelsinternational.com.

Sustainable development and the hospitality industry

The hospitality industry encompasses a wide range of different types of businesses, both with respect to the products they offer to customers and aspects such as size and ownership arrangements. A small independent restaurant operated by a husband and wife, in which the husband's domain is the kitchen and the wife interacts with diners, serves them food and drinks, takes care of reservations and payments and so on, belongs to this industry. Marriott International is an American hospitality company that manages and franchises hotels and other types of lodging facilities. In 2016, Marriott merged with Starwood to create the world's largest hotel company. This company covers about 30 brands and more than 5000 properties worldwide, which amounts to more than a million rooms. This international hotel company is also part of the hospitality industry. Restaurants and hotels are generally considered the two key areas of this industry. However, 'hospitality industry' is often also used as an umbrella term for not only these two sectors but also businesses and professionals operating in entertainment and recreation, such as theme parks and casinos; travel service provision, such as cruise lines and sightseeing companies; and assembly and event management, such as convention centres and exhibitions. In turn, the hospitality industry is part of the wider tourism industry, which also includes businesses such as travel agencies, (online) booking companies and airlines.

This heterogeneity of the hospitality industry and the ambiguity regarding delineation of its borders make it difficult to provide a precise assessment of its contribution to (achieving) sustainable development. As indicated in the

Introduction to this book, providing a full overview of all sustainability aspects linked to this industry and the (technical) details of addressing them in the particular contexts created by the specific circumstances of the full range of different companies involved is beyond the scope of this book. However, in general terms, the hospitality industry could make a contribution in two distinct ways: (1) reducing the negative impact(s) of this industry, and (2) increasing the positive impact(s) of this industry.

The negative impact of the hospitality industry

Tourism can be linked to a range of negative impacts from a sustainable development perspective. The one that stands out is greenhouse gas emissions associated with this industry. Most of these greenhouse gas emissions are linked to travelling, as a result of most tourists either using a car or an airplane to reach their destination. With more and more people preferring and being able to afford the latter mode of transport, air travel has already increased significantly and will continue to increase rapidly in years to come, which amounts to equal increases in emissions of particles and gases such as CO_2, hydrocarbons, nitrogen oxides, lead and more. Consequently, air travel contributes significantly to pollution and climate change. The current contribution of aviation to climate change is estimated somewhere between 5% and 10%. However, the actual size of this problem becomes clear if you realise that, if one accounts for current predictions regarding population growth, income growth and technological developments, around the years 2050/2060 greenhouse gas emissions linked to air travel would equal almost all the greenhouse gas emissions we can afford if we want to limit global warming to $2°$ C (Peeters, 2017), as agreed upon in the so-called Paris Agreement. In other words, if we want to stick to the Paris Agreement and these predictions prove accurate, we would need to reduce the contribution to climate change of other industries, sectors and activities, such as those associated with (constructing and heating) buildings, manufacturing, other forms of transport and agriculture, to . . . zero!

Obviously, given that airlines and airports are usually not considered to be part of the hospitality industry, one could argue that emissions linked to flying are not formally the responsibility of this industry. However, a lot of us do step into an airplane to spend our holiday in a hotel or resort that is a formal part of the hospitality industry. Business people and academics do often travel to meetings and conferences organised in and hosted by conference hotels and convention centres that are integral to this industry. What is more, a lot of the products offered to their guests by hospitality businesses and professionals, for instance that tender piece of steak from New Zealand or strawberries on the menu in wintertime in a restaurant in Europe or the US, have travelled across our globe by airplane to get there. So have a lot of the materials used for constructing, furnishing and decorating the broad range of facilities that together shape the hospitality industry. In the end, it really does not matter who is to blame for specific emissions from a legal or industry delineation perspective. The fact remains that the tourism and hospitality industries, but also the transport and agriculture sectors, are intertwined in many ways and all of them, as do we consumers, have a role to play in reducing greenhouse gas emissions. Achieving sustainable development is our joint responsibility and the hospitality industry plays a crucial role in this specific negative impact of human activity on our planet and (thus) in mitigating it.

However, air travel is certainly not the only way in which this industry is involved with negative impacts of human activity on our planet and people. For instance, quite a few hospitality establishments are located in pristine natural environments across our globe. Roads have been constructed cutting through wilderness to make them accessible. These establishments often attract large numbers of tourists and not all of them make a concerted effort to minimise their negative impact on the local ecosystem and the remaining wildlife. Obviously, this ecosystem has already been impacted during construction of those hospitality facilities. However, negative impacts are not necessarily limited to the local ecosystem. The construction of any hospitality facility, regardless of where it is located, requires significant natural resources, and sometimes materials used are not only scarce but can also be linked to a range of negative consequences throughout their supply chain.

Potential negative consequences of hospitality businesses are not limited to the construction phase and also not to environmental consequences. Some of these aspects are discussed in more detail in the next chapter but it is important to note here that consumption of natural resources continues once a hospitality business becomes operational. In fact, the hospitality industry is known for its high consumption of energy and water. It is also known for generating high amounts of waste. A number of companies in this industry focus on providing guests with comfort and luxury, which is quite often translated in focusing on *oversupplying* guests. A typical example would be the copious amounts of bathroom amenities provided to guests of hotels, resorts and other accommodation facilities. Many of those are packaged individually in plastic or small bottles. Once a guest has used a little bit of the bar of soap or bottle of hair conditioning lotion, the remainder of the bar and contents of the bottle, including the bottle itself, are disposed of by housekeeping and replaced with brand – pun intended – new supplies. Another typical example is serving guests food and drinks as a buffet. A buffet is defined by the Oxford English Dictionary as a meal consisting of several dishes from which guests serve themselves and the online version of this dictionary includes the following sentence as an example of how to use the word 'buffet': 'The best meal of the day was, without doubt, breakfast, which is served as a buffet, but is essentially a feast of 20 or so heaving tables offering more dishes than anyone could sample in a week.' Unfortunately, this sentence actually accurately describes the situation in quite a few hospitality establishments. This generates enormous amounts of food waste. What is more, one could question whether oversupplying your guests really equals caring for them and treating them well. Within the context of food and drinks, from a health perspective, it certainly does not.

Which brings us to the people component of sustainable development. Obviously, the hospitality industry is very much people-oriented; at the core of this industry lays the relationship between hosts and guests, the interaction between people. Therefore, one would expect this industry to focus on the social dimension of sustainable development in trying to make a contribution, for instance through caring for the well-being of employees and guests, and engaging with local communities. In reality, this industry, especially the hotel and restaurant sectors, has a rather questionable reputation when it comes to working conditions for and remuneration of its employees. As indicated in the previous paragraph, you could also question whether caring for the well-being of guests really equals carelessly oversupplying them with food, drinks and amenities. Finally, whereas tourism is often ascribed the power to stimulate local economies, the hospitality industry is not really known for its active contribution to an equal division of wealth across people around our globe. In fact, examples of globally operating chains putting independent, local entrepreneurs out of business are widespread. Simultaneously, this industry is increasingly seen by those who have already acquired more than their fair share of wealth as an interesting investment opportunity and environment to increase brand or market value as a means to further increase (the value of) their share(s).

In reality, the global hospitality industry is more and more turning into an arena in which high net worth individuals and institutional investors, such as insurance companies, real estate investment trusts and private equity funds, compete for money instead of focusing on, and sometimes at the expense of, the interaction between people within businesses that are intertwined with local communities. As with the environmental aspects, this particular aspect and some of the other aspects of the link between the hospitality industry and the social dimension of sustainable development are discussed in more detail in later chapters. However, within the context of this preliminary assessment it would be fair to conclude that the hospitality industry could make a significant contribution to (achieving) sustainable development by (purposely) reducing or avoiding some of the negative consequences associated with its (current) ways of operating.

Reducing this negative impact

There are numerous certification schemes, checklists and labels that hospitality businesses and professionals could use as guidelines and inspiration to reduce their negative impacts from a sustainable development perspective. More importantly, numerous hospitality businesses and professionals actually use them. What is more, both scientific and popular (science) publications and media report on these efforts extensively, as well as on best practices related to specific sustainability measures and initiatives. Together, this creates a wealth of information available to all hospitality businesses and professionals to figure out which schemes, measures, initiatives and solutions would fit their specific circumstances. Finally, practitioners in some sectors have also joined forces in various ways, for instance with respect to exchanging information and jointly defining ambitions and setting standards for (specific) sustainability aspects and measures. The International Tourism Partnership (ITP) is a typical example of such a collaboration. A number of the world's biggest and most influential hotel chains have joined this initiative and have partnered with KPMG and the World Travel & Tourism Council (WTTC) to set up the Hotel Carbon Measurement Initiative (HCMI): a shared methodology for measuring and communicating greenhouse gas emissions of hotels.

Combined with the oftentimes significant enthusiasm and drive of individual and groups of hospitality professionals, both management and staff, all of this has resulted in numerous hospitality companies making quite some progress already in reducing their negative impacts. The assortment of measures that some of these companies have introduced is impressive. We all know the bathroom signs indicating that if you do not put your towel on the floor, the accommodation provider is going to assume that you will use it again without it being laundered first. As trivial as this simple measure may seem, it actually saves a lot of energy, water and pollution linked to laundry detergents. A lot of hotels, resorts, bed & breakfasts, restaurants, theatres and theme parks now include vegetarian and/or vegan dishes on their menus and use local and organic produce to prepare their dishes. A number of companies have introduced a range of measures to save energy and water. Some of the facilities in the hospitality industry have been purposely designed and constructed to reduce or even completely avoid greenhouse gas emissions. More and more companies carefully select suppliers and materials they use based on sustainability considerations, also linked to the social component of sustainable development. Others have made an effort to employ people with a so-called distance to the labour market and have improved working conditions and remuneration for staff. Finally, some hospitality companies have literally started to share their space(s) with local stakeholders. For instance, Zoku Amsterdam has created so-called social spaces: communal working spaces that can be used by staff, guests *and* local entrepreneurs and residents.

Even though some of these measures by some of these companies might not be the result of intrinsic motivation of decision-makers involved but rather represent a reaction to public and/or regulatory pressures, the fact remains that today's average hospitality business could be argued to be less unsustainable than 10 or 20 years ago. Some of this progress might have been lost through an increase in the number of customers served by this industry, as well as the wider tourism industry and thus also air travel and disturbance of ecosystems, but it would be unfair to say that nothing has been done (yet) to reduce the negative impact(s) of the hospitality industry. Simultaneously, as the remainder of this chapter and the subsequent chapters will show, there is still a world to be won.

Corporate Social Responsibility, reporting and transparency

As indicated by Jones *et al.*, the truth is that, throughout the hospitality industry, 'the concept of sustainability [still] provides a teasing paradox' (2016, p. 37). Sustainability now plays an important role at the operational, the tactical and the strategic level for most companies in this industry. At the operational level, the ultimate customer experience offered to (paying) guests, visitors, diners, clients or customers more often than not incorporates sustainability measures to at least some extent. Sometimes this is limited to trivial measures such as the well-known cards in hotel bathrooms with messages about reusing towels, sometimes this has completely changed the ultimate experience. A menu with only vegetarian dishes would be a typical example of the latter. At the tactical level, quite a few hospitality businesses and professionals include sustainability aspects in their marketing messages, even though this is often limited to referring to a specific label or certification. Simultaneously, specific sustainability measures have become business-as-usual because they represent a good business case. Some (corporate) clients would not book a room in your hotel or visit your premises if you could not prove to live up to a certain minimum sustainability standard, for instance through qualifying for the very same sustainability labels or certifications mentioned earlier. Other sustainability measures simply save money through saving water or energy. Combined with pressure from the general public and the logical desire to avoid possible legal challenges, all of this has resulted in sustainability now representing something that you simply have to address as a hospitality business or professional.

In fact, especially sizeable companies, and those that are listed on the stock exchange, have developed (extensive) sustainability policies, usually as part of so-called Corporate Social Responsibility (CSR) or Corporate Citizenship (CC) programmes. Most of these companies also explicitly report on their environmental, social and (business) economic impact – the well-known three Ps (people, planet, profit), following the Triple Bottom Line reporting principles introduced by John Elkington (1997), in their annual reports or special CSR reports. This is usually done in the form of numerous tables and figures, which are accompanied by beautifully worded high-minded long-term goals.

Simultaneously, many of these same companies still offer experiences to their guests, visitors, diners, clients and customers based on oversupplying them. King-size, luxury, seduction and excitement are not only the principles on which many of these experiences are based but also the terms often used to advertise them. And, ultimately, despite some of the hopeful and promising messages included in CSR reports and displayed on websites, the one goal that prevails over all others is to increase profits and market share. Even though many companies 'stress their commitment to sustainability and to integrating it into their core business strategy [they do so] while pursuing continuing growth which makes a range of demands on environmental [and social] resources' (Jones *et al.*, 2016, p. 37). This also means that some companies engage in greenwashing to attract customers that value sustainability.

Interestingly, others actually engage in the opposite of greenwashing, i.e., greenhushing (Font *et al.*, 2017). This phenomenon relates to purposely understating your efforts with respect to sustainability measures and initiatives out of a fear of scaring off potential customers. For some reason, many hospitality professionals, especially in the hotel industry, are convinced that customers are predominantly driven by hedonic and gain motives (Melissen *et al.*, 2016). In other words, they believe that customers do not want to be bothered with sustainability measures and initiatives, and simply want to enjoy their stay, holiday, evening out or visit offered to them by the hospitality company without being confronted with possible negative impacts linked to their decisions regarding consuming that particular hospitality product, service or experience and the way they do so. All of this leads to a situation in which businesses and professionals officially state they are committed to sustainable development but actually go out of their way to either overstate or understate their actual efforts and impacts, depending on what is considered *smart business* within a specific context. In turn, as indicated earlier in the chapter, this leads to consumers ending up rather sceptical regarding the motives of those claiming to be or act sustainable. In turn, this cynicism is then often interpreted by hospitality providers as *not caring about* or *not wanting to be bothered with* sustainability measures and initiatives.

CASE 1.2

Greenhushing?

Introduction

One of the authors of this book has recently supervised a graduation student whose thesis focuses on the perception of guests towards sustainability, based on the case of a 4-star hotel with 230 rooms. The hotel has a Green Key certificate. Green Key is a voluntary eco-label for establishments within the tourism industry. Based on the standards set by Green Key, the hotel has implemented sustainable practices in terms of people, planet and profit, e.g., energy efficient devices.

So what?

These practices are not directly visible or promoted to guests, neither is there explicit mention of the Green Key label for instance through a plaque near the front door of the hotel's premises. It was also not known how guests would respond to these practices, if they'd notice any changes and if so, if they'd appreciate them. Therefore, after discussing this with one member of management, the graduation student focused on assessing whether guests had noticed (the impact of) these sustainable measures. He found that the majority of guests had not. Guests also did not think these measures had influenced their level of comfort during their stay.

What is more striking though, or perhaps shocking is a better word, is that during the research the student discovered that almost all employees and even most members of management at the establishment were not aware of the Green Key certification of the hotel. As it turned out, the decision to pursue this certification, and the application process itself, represented topics that were, so far, only discussed at the headquarters of the chain that this particular hotel belongs to. Measures, such as the need to install new devices, were communicated by headquarters to all individual establishments but the background for these measures – for instance, reducing energy use and living up to the Green Key certification standards – were not. If there ever was an example of green-hushing... or is it?

Obviously, transparency is a key ingredient and precondition for achieving sustainable development, even at the level of an individual company. It is impossible to decide on the most sustainable alternative without incorporating all possible outcomes, also from a social and environmental perspective, and the perspectives of and impacts on all relevant stakeholders. Unfortunately, the previous paragraph describes a situation that is quite different; a vicious circle leading to limited transparency about actual motives, efforts and results, and a situation in which decisions regarding sustainability measures and initiatives are heavily influenced by purely (business) economic motives. This paradox is not unique to the hospitality industry. Companies in other industries also struggle with simultaneously meeting sustainable development demands and the demands of operating and surviving in the free market. Many of them need to satisfy shareholders who expect a reasonable return on their investment. Acquiring funds for investing in new facilities or maintaining existing ones becomes a lot harder if you do not make enough profit. Most customers are not willing to pay extra for more sustainable products, services and experiences and would pick the cheapest one if and when offered alternatives of equal quality.

We will return to these so-called self-reinforcing mechanisms of our current socio-economic system in more detail later in this book, but here it is important to note that the hospitality industry could be argued to be especially vulnerable to these mechanisms. An industry with a core product, hospitality experiences, that is often based on concepts such as luxury, indulgence and oversupply might find it especially difficult to change this product into more sustainable alternatives. A big portion of this industry consists of small, independent companies with limited financial means and access to new insights and technologies, which makes it even more difficult to make these changes. Finally, for some reason, over time, the relationship that lies at the heart of the hospitality industry, the relationship between host and guest, seems to have evolved into a relationship that is based on assumptions about *the Other* rather than one based on transparency, and open and direct communication about the motives, values and preferences of both parties involved. Consequently, the actual host–guest relationship between a number of hospitality businesses and their (potential) customers seems to act as a barrier rather than a catalyst for furthering sustainability in this industry (Cavagnaro *et al.*, 2018).

The status quo and reasons for not accepting it

In their recent reflections on the state of sustainability in the hospitality industry, Jones *et al.* conclude that 'definitions of sustainability within the hospitality industry can be interpreted as being constructed around business imperatives rather than an ongoing commitment to sustainability', that 'materiality and external assurance are not treated comprehensively' and 'that the concept of sustainable consumption and any critique of the industry's commitment to economic growth are conspicuous by their absence' (2016, p. 36). Based on the preliminary assessment of the current contribution of the hospitality industry to achieving sustainable development presented in this first chapter, this rather harsh conclusion unfortunately also seems to be rather accurate. Despite an abundance of certification schemes and labels, dedicated partnerships and beautifully worded high-minded long-term goals in CSR reports and on company websites, sustainability principles have not yet been fully integrated into the core business strategies, tactics and operations of most hospitality businesses and professionals. There is no doubt that a lot of progress has been made with respect to making this industry less unsustainable than it was a few decades ago and that quite a few individual businesses and professionals are highly motivated to move further forward, but, overall, this industry now seems stuck in what Benn *et al.* (2014) refer to as the efficiency phase of organisational change towards sustainability.

The remainder of this book is dedicated to exploring avenues to break this deadlock. There are two reasons why this is so important.

First, despite the range of sustainability measures and initiatives already introduced to date, this industry still negatively impacts our environment quite significantly. Even though this industry plays an important role in our economies and thus in generating income for quite few people, the way in which it does so not always qualifies as sustainable from a social perspective, especially in relation to improving the quality of lives of *all* people, both across our globe and in the long run. Therefore, if new measures, initiatives, innovations and concepts could be introduced that would assist in having the hospitality industry generate the same or more societal value while for instance improving remuneration and working conditions for hospitality workers, negatively influencing the lives of less people across our globe, and consuming less natural resources, this would already amount to a (much) more significant contribution to achieving sustainable development of our societies.

Second, there is no reason why the hospitality industry's contribution to sustainable development would have to stop at reducing its (direct) negative impacts. This industry could also create a number of positive impacts. As indicated by Melissen (2018), there are at least three reasons why the hospitality industry could be argued to be in a perfect position to move beyond minimising its own negative impacts and actually serve as a catalyst for achieving sustainable development of our societies:

1. Hospitality experiences are offered by a wide variety of businesses and professionals, 'ranging from powerful and influential globally operating [. . .] chains to local, independent businesses that are completely inter-twined with local communities' (Melissen, 2018, p.155). Consequently, if all of these companies would truly promote sustainable development (goals and principles), this would stimulate, support and influence (the actions of) a wide range of stakeholders at all levels of the so-called 'global-local nexus' (Saarinen, 2006, p. 1134) involved with sustainable develop-ment. This industry could thus serve as a crucial partner for all parties and initiatives that focus on the systemic nature of sustainable development, without being hampered by artificial boundaries such as industry delinea-tion and country borders. The example of air travel discussed earlier is a typical example of this. Officially, air travel is not part of the hospitality industry. However, the hospitality and tourism industries are inextricably linked and the hospitality industry would automatically (have to) play a crucial role in any initiative to address this problem.

2. Businesses and professionals providing hospitality experiences to custo-mers, regardless of whether they are operating independently or as part of a bigger chain, 'are automatically linked to local social, economic and environmental systems' (Melissen, 2018, p. 154). They employ, and thus create work and income for, local residents; they sell their products to, and thus influence the behaviour of, visitors to a destination (and thus the impact of those visitors on that destination); they buy supplies from local suppliers; they consume/impact local natural resources/ecosystems; and so on. Therefore, these businesses and professionals are *natural* stakeholders and partners in sustainable development of local and regional social, environmental and economic systems.

3. Hospitality experiences are consumed by almost all of us. As such, the businesses and professionals offering them to us and the way in which they do so could influence the perspectives of a significant portion of our world's population, especially given that most of these experiences are

based on direct interaction between host/provider and guest/consumer. This interaction usually takes place in pleasurable circumstances. Most hospitality experiences are designed to make you happy, to have you enjoy consuming them. You could not ask for better circumstances to discuss sustainability or to try out sustainable products and services. If hospitality businesses and professionals could show us, consumers, that sustainability can be enjoyable and that sustainable products and services can be perfect alternatives to unsustainable ones, the positive impact of the hospitality industry on sustainable development could move far beyond simply minimising its own negative impacts. The hospitality industry could actually play a crucial role in showing us how to change our behaviours into more sustainable ones without that having to lead to a lower quality of life. They could prove to us that sustainable products and services do not necessarily have to be more expensive, less fun, less tasty or of lesser quality, thus stimulating us to start using more sustainable products and services in our daily lives as well.

Together, these three aspects imply that the hospitality industry's contribution need not be limited to further decreasing its own direct negative impact. The hospitality industry could actually play a crucial role in achieving sustainable development of our societies and a transition towards a sustainable alternative for our current socio-economic system. The subsequent chapters are dedicated to exploring how this industry could realise this potential.

SUMMARY

Based on reading this chapter, we hope you will understand and remember the following:

- Sustainability is understood in different ways by different parties and – therefore – sometimes misused.
- The concept of sustainable development knows a long history.
- Sustainable development is development that meets the needs of the present without compromising the ability of future generations to meet their own needs.
- There is a need to drastically change the way we use our planet to satisfy our needs.
- The hospitality industry could make a contribution to sustainable development by:
  - reducing the negative impact(s) of this industry;
  - increasing the positive impact(s) of this industry.

- Air travel is one of largest contributors to climate change, and this will continue to become a more significant problem in years to come.
- Hospitality businesses negatively affect the environment by using too many resources, such as water and energy, or creating too much waste.
- Sustainability policies are usually part of Corporate Social Responsibility (CSR) programmes and reported on via the Triple Bottom Line (people, planet, profit).
- Some companies deliberately overstate or understate sustainability efforts, which is referred to as greenwashing and greenhushing respectively.
- Transparency is key to avoiding consumer scepticism and cynicism.
- Despite all of its efforts, the hospitality industry is stuck in the efficiency phase of organisational change towards sustainability.
- Three reasons why the hospitality industry could actually serve as a catalyst for achieving sustainable development of our societies are:
  - hospitality experiences are offered by a wide variety of businesses and professionals;
  - these businesses and professionals are natural stakeholders in local and regional social, environmental and economic systems;
  - hospitality experiences are consumed by almost all of us.

FOOD FOR THOUGHT

Based on the content of this chapter, the following questions, challenges and topics could serve as interesting starting points for further discussion:

- Think of ways that sustainability has played/plays a role in your life so far.
- Could you name a few hospitality businesses or experiences that represent good examples of how to implement sustainability?
- Think of your own consumption behaviour as a guest, tourist or traveller. What changes could or should you make, from a sustainable development perspective?
- Would you want to make those changes if it meant you could live longer on this planet?

References

Benn, S., Dunphy, D. & Griffiths, A. (2014). *Organizational change for corporate sustainability* (3rd ed.) New York: Routledge.

Cavagnaro, E., Düweke, A. & Melissen, F. (2018). 'The host–guest relationship is the key to sustainable hospitality: Lessons learned from a Dutch case study'. *Hospitality & Society*, 8(1), 23–44.

Elkington, J. (1997). *Cannibals with forks: The triple bottom line of 21st century business*. Oxford: Capstone.

Font, X., Elgammal, I. & Lamond, I. (2017). 'Greenhushing: the deliberate under communicating of sustainability practices by tourism businesses'. *Journal of Sustainable Tourism*, 25(7), 1007–1023.

Jones, P., Hillier, D. & Comfort, D. (2016). 'Sustainability in the hospitality industry: Some personal reflections on corporate challenges and research agendas'. *International Journal of Contemporary Hospitality Management*, 28 (1), 36–67.

Meadows, D.H., Meadows, D.L., Randers, J. & Behrens III, W. (Club of Rome) (1972). *The limits to growth: A report for the Club of Rome's project on the predicament of mankind*. New York: Universe Books.

Melissen, F. (2018). 'Hotels and sustainability'. In R.C. Wood (ed.) *Hotel accommodation management* (pp. 152–163). New York: Routledge.

Melissen, F., Cavagnaro, E., Damen, M. & Düweke, A. (2016). 'Is the hotel industry prepared to face the challenge of sustainable development?' *Journal of Vacation Marketing*, 22(3), 227–238.

Peeters, P. (2017). *Tourism's impact on climate change and its mitigation challenges: How can tourism become 'climate sustainable'?* (dissertation). Delft: Delft University of Technology.

Saarinen, J. (2006). 'Traditions of sustainability in tourism studies'. *Annals of Tourism Research*, 33(4), 1121–1140.

United Nations' World Commission on Environment and Development (UNWCED) (Brundtland Commission) (1987). *Our common future (The Brundtland Report)*. Oxford: Oxford University Press.

CHAPTER

2 Technology versus behaviour

Introduction

As indicated earlier, authors of numerous other publications have already addressed (most of) the details of particular technologies and processes that could play an important role in reducing the negative environmental (and sometimes also social) impact of the hospitality industry. A recent example of such a publication is the third edition of *Sustainability in the Hospitality Industry: Principles of sustainable operations* by Legrand, Sloan and Chen (2017). This chapter reviews some of the key topics addressed by Legrand *et al.*: energy management, waste management, water management, sustainable food, and building (materials and furnishing). The reason for doing so is neither to criticise this particular book nor to prove that we could do a better job of providing a full review of all relevant topics, technologies and processes; we probably could not. In fact, we highly recommend publications like the one by Legrand *et al.* (2017) for exploring specific sustainability topics, technologies and processes in more detail. These topics are discussed here within the context of the particular call for action that forms the common thread running through all chapters of *our* book. Reviewing these topics through addressing some of the basic problems and possible solutions highlighted by these authors allows for linking them to the three reasons why the hospitality industry could serve as a catalyst for achieving sustainable development of our societies, as identified in the previous chapter.

The 'Big Five' of sustainable hospitality operations

Typically, hospitality companies, such as hotels, restaurants, theme parks and theatres, consume a lot of water and energy and generate a lot of waste. A key ingredient of almost any hospitality experience offered to customers by these companies is to provide food and drinks as an integral part of that experience. The setting in which these experiences are staged are usually purposely created for doing so. Constructing and maintaining these facilities not only requires huge amounts of materials but also energy and water, and the choices made during the design and construction phases to a large extent determine energy and water use during the operation stage. Together, these five elements – energy, waste, water, food/drinks, and the building (including its materials and furnishing) – are responsible for a significant part of the negative environmental (and sometimes social) impact of the hospitality industry. Therefore, any attempt to make the hospitality industry more sustainable needs to at least address these issues.

Energy and greenhouse gas emissions

Even if we disregard the hospitality industry's link to air travel and other forms of transportation used by its customers to travel to and from hospitality facilities, this industry is still directly responsible for a significant portion of global energy use and greenhouse gas emissions. As Legrand *et al.* (2017) explain, operating buildings can be linked to about 40% of total energy use and a third of all greenhouse gas emissions. Hospitality facilities are created for staging hospitality experiences for customers and, as discussed in the previous chapter, many of these experiences are based on concepts such as comfort, luxury and oversupply. Consequently, energy use for the typical hospitality facility is rather high compared to other types of buildings. Just consider the amount of energy needed to cool a casino on a tropical island or to heat a hotel in a ski resort. Obviously, energy is also needed for heating water for showering in hotel rooms or pools, and hot tubs in spa and wellness centres. Preparing the food that is served as an integral part of the hospitality experience staged for guests, diners and visitors of hotels, restaurants, theatres and theme parks also uses considerable amounts of energy, especially if you also consider the energy needed for transporting the ingredients to the hospitality facility and storing them at the facility in a way that prevents them from spoiling.

Consequently, the hospitality industry's carbon footprint is high, which means that it contributes significantly to global climate change and all related (short-term and long-term) environmental, social and economic damages. Therefore, Legrand *et al.* (2017) highlight a number of interesting technologies, processes and measures for decreasing this footprint. Ultimately, they identify two key areas for reducing the hospitality industry's carbon footprint: (1) using renewable instead of non-renewable energy sources, and (2) reducing the overall amount of energy used.

Greenhouse gas emissions are the result of using fossil fuels, such as gas, coal and oil, to generate energy. Hospitality companies can rely on these non-renewable energy sources in two ways. First, they might use fossil fuels themselves, for instance gas to heat the building in which a casino is located or petrol for a lorry used by staff responsible for keeping the vast garden that surrounds the castle in which a luxurious hotel is located in picture-perfect condition. Second, they might use electricity, for instance for heating water used by guests in a resort for showering or for induction cooktops, electric ovens and fridges in restaurants. In most parts of our world, this electricity is generated in power plants that use gas or coal. Through using this electricity, hospitality companies thus rely on the fossil fuels used by these power plants.

Therefore, one of the most obvious ways for hospitality companies to reduce their carbon footprint is to switch to electricity that is generated using renewable energy sources, such as wind, hydro or solar power. In some countries, more and more power plants are using these renewable energy sources and utility companies offer a choice to end-users to switch to so-called green electricity. In other countries, it might prove difficult to find a utility company who can guarantee that the electricity you use is actually generated in an environmentally responsible way.

In those situations, and also with respect to the fossil fuels used in daily operations, a hospitality company would have to rely on local solutions for decreasing its carbon footprint. Legrand *et al.* (2017) describe a number of these solutions, such as:

- Using solar energy to generate electricity, mechanical power, heat and lighting.
- Using nature to light, warm and cool your facilities, for instance by installing roof light wells, planting trees that protect you from the sun in the summer and allowing the sun to warm your buildings in winter, designing your buildings in such a way that cooling breezes can ventilate and cool the air in your facilities, and so on.
- Wind turbines to generate electricity.
- Using geothermal resources to either directly heat or cool your facilities and water or to generate electricity.

Some of these solutions could be applied at an individual hospitality facility, whereas others might involve teaming up with local suppliers, such as local farmers who have the space to install solar panels or wind turbines. In some countries or regions, you can now buy your electricity directly from such local green electricity providers. Obviously, to ensure that you reduce your carbon footprint as much as possible, you would need to switch the heating system in your hospitality facility from one that uses gas to one that uses electricity. For heating water, you could switch from gas burners to boilers linked to solar panels that are used to heat the water. In the kitchen, you would have to switch from gas-powered cooktops and ovens to, for instance, induction cooktops and electric ovens.

Obviously, regardless of the specific technologies involved in supplying the energy needed for operating a hospitality company, one of the most direct ways to reduce one's carbon footprint is to reduce the total amount of energy needed. Insulation, window sizes, materials used for walls and roofs, and so on, all play a key role in the ultimate amount of energy needed. And finally, if all else fails and it proves impossible to further reduce the carbon footprint of a specific facility, you might engage in carbon offsetting. In essence, carbon offsetting comes down to compensating for your greenhouse gas emissions, for instance through (financially) supporting organisations that plant trees or help others to reduce their carbon footprint.

Books like the one by Legrand *et al.* (2017) and a wide range of other publications, as well as dedicated websites, certification schemes and initiatives, such as the Hotel Carbon Measurement Initiative mentioned in Chapter 1, offer individual hospitality businesses and professionals a wealth of information, suggestions, checklists, tips and tricks that could assist them in making the most of the wealth of solutions already *out there*. In fact, for almost any practical situation imaginable, a solution based on applying a specific technology or process is already known that could very well reduce the carbon footprint linked to that situation significantly, sometimes even to the extent that you could apply a local solution that would actually amount to operating in such a way that you generate more (green!) energy than you consume or absorb more greenhouse gases than you emit. The latter is called a negative carbon footprint.

As indicated in the previous chapter, fortunately, a number of hospitality businesses and professionals already apply some of these solutions. Some hospitality facilities have been designed and constructed in such a way that their carbon footprint is zero or even negative. A number of existing buildings have been renovated to reduce their carbon footprint, for instance within the context of the EU-funded project Nearly Zero Energy Hotels (neZEH). This project ran from 2013 to 2016 and provided assistance to committed hoteliers to turn their hospitality facilities into nearly energy-neutral buildings. A nice example of an individual company taking responsibility for its contribution to global climate change is Le Pain Quotidien, an international chain of bakery-restaurants. They started their quest to become carbon neutral at their (more than 40) New York- and Connecticut-based restaurants in the United States with calculating the carbon footprint of those restaurants, and reviewing all areas of their operations that contributed to this footprint, to create a full understanding of what they could do to reduce it. Based on that analysis, all lighting in their facilities is now based on LED technology and they have invested in more energy-efficient kitchen equipment. They have also decided to offset their remaining carbon footprint by supporting a charity that focuses on reducing greenhouse gas emissions. Le Pain Quotidien has picked a project in Uganda, which is dedicated to making cleaner energy accessible to local communities. In 2016, Le Pain Quotidien reported that their US based restaurants are now operating carbon neutral and they aim to do the same for all of their other restaurants across the globe by 2020.

Sometimes, you really do not need complicated technologies or offsetting to reduce or mitigate local greenhouse gas emissions. Why would thermostats in hospitality facilities need to be set at more than 20° C or even 18° C? StayOkay Hostels in the Netherlands participates in the national so-called *Warmetruiendag* (Warm Sweater Day) each year. To raise awareness for climate change, like at many other companies and organisations, at their national headquarters they turn down the thermostats that day and staff put on warm sweaters. One degree lower on the thermostat means 6% less energy used and 6% less greenhouse gas emission.

By now, almost all hospitality providers across our globe have introduced bathroom signs indicating that if you do not put your towel on the floor, they will assume you will use it again and will not wash it. This may not be the most technologically advanced and *sexy* measure you could come up with but it still saves energy and greenhouse gas emissions.

Waste and pollution

Climate change, as a result of greenhouse gas emissions, represents a problem that most of us are fully aware of and that receives a lot of attention in both scientific and popular publications and media coverage. However, it is certainly not the only problem that needs to be addressed from a sustainable development perspective. Waste and pollution, with the latter often being the direct result of the first, represent two of those *other* problems.

Our modern-day society has organised production and consumption of the products, services and experiences we crave in a wasteful and polluting way. Just consider the garbage patches, sometimes referred to as plastic soup, in our oceans. These patches basically represent areas in our oceans where, through currents, huge concentrations of plastic (particles), chemical sludge and all kinds of other debris have amassed. A study recently published by Geyer *et al.* (2017) concluded that, of the close to 10 billion tons of plastic that we, humans, have produced and consumed over the course of the last seven decades, close to 7 billion tons are no longer used. Less than 10% of these discarded plastics have been recycled and another 12% have been incinerated. This means that the remaining 6 billion tons or so are now littering and polluting our oceans, lakes and soil. Shockingly, scientists actually expect the total weight of plastics in our oceans to exceed the total weight of fish in those same oceans within a few decades. These plastics end up in the stomachs of animals and, through our food chains, also in people's stomachs. Many of these plastic particles have picked up an array of other pollutants, such as PCBs and DDT, along the way. Needless to say, these plastics are not just an aesthetic problem but also represent a significant and growing health problem for all living organisms, including humans, on our planet.

Unfortunately, the incineration of plastics often only adds to this problem. Many of the facilities used for incineration of waste, not just plastics but also a number of other types of waste, are responsible for emissions of particularly toxic substances, such as dioxins and heavy metals, into the air. These substances harm us humans and all other living organisms not only through the air we breathe but also through ending up in water and soil, and, ultimately, once again, in our food chains. The same applies to landfills, which have the added 'bonus' of also generating greenhouse gases, such as methane.

Obviously, these represent just a few examples of the seemingly endless number of ways in which our production and consumption patterns are associated with waste and pollution. We will spare you, our reader, a full rendering of all ways in which these patterns can cause and already have caused landscapes to change, acidification of land and water, biodiversity loss and health problems, just to name a few of the many interrelated problems and risks. However, it is important to mention another side to this coin. Waste is not just linked to pollution; it is also linked to resource use. Given that Earth's resources are limited, we cannot afford to waste them, even if we would do so in a way that does not lead to pollution. We actually already use more resources, not just oil, coal and gas but also wood, precious metals and so on, than Earth can provide in the long run. If we combine predicted population growth and our current production and consumption patterns, we would actually need two Earths by 2030 to support these patterns!

As with greenhouse gas emissions, today's hospitality industry is responsible for a considerable proportion of our world's waste problem. Whilst most hospitality facilities do not emit or leak pollutants into land, water and air directly, they do generate a lot of waste. As indicated by Legrand *et al.* (2017), waste generated by the hospitality industry broadly falls into one of two categories: (1) wet or organic waste, and (2) dry waste, such as plastics, glass, paper and electronic waste. The first category is mostly made up of food waste and represents nearly half of all waste generated by this industry. We will return to this crucial topic in more detail later in this section.

A typical example of the second category has already been discussed in Chapter 1: the waste generated by hotels, resorts and other accommodation facilities through providing guests with copious amounts of bathroom amenities, often individually packaged in small plastic or glass bottles, tubes and so on. However, the typical hospitality company also generates a lot of paper waste, for instance through printing reservations and bills but also work schedules for staff, and electronic waste. The latter is linked to the enormous amount of electronic equipment used in hospitality facilities, ranging from lamps and TV and computer screens to vacuum cleaners, toasters, washing machines, hair dryers, dishwashers, and cooling and freezing equipment. Many of these appliances could potentially be reused, refurbished or recycled. In reality though, most electronic waste in our world is traded, transported and processed illegally and in environmentally irresponsible ways. Unfortunately, appliances discarded by the hospitality industry are no exception to this rule.

Technological solutions can bring relief for some of the problems associated with waste and pollution, also in the hospitality industry. For instance, information technology could assist in reducing the amount of paper used. However, most of these problems need to be addressed in different ways. In fact, many of them represent a choice. Is it necessary to install a TV in every hotel room? Why use individually packaged soap bars and small bottles of shampoo when you could also use dispensers that can be refilled? LED lighting not only saves energy but also has a longer (service) lifetime. Why could curtains in hotel rooms, or those used on stage in theatres for that matter, not be made of recycled textiles? The same goes for bed sheets, towels, banquet linens, and so on. It is not that difficult to decide on staff uniforms that can easily be recycled. The same goes for those curtains, towels, bed sheets, and so on. For almost anything used in hospitality operations, suppliers can be found who can provide less hazardous, less toxic, less wasteful and less resource-intensive alternatives. Sometimes, all that is needed is to look for them. Consequently, the list of choices that influence the amount and types of waste and pollution generated by hospitality companies is almost endless. In fact, for almost any practical situation imaginable, various solutions are already known, and available to hospitality businesses and professionals, that could very well reduce the amount of waste and the pollution that they generate, either directly or indirectly. Most of these solutions do not require advanced technologies or significant investments; they require making different choices.

Water

One could argue that the need to make different choices also applies to another major area of concern from a sustainable development perspective: droughts and (clean drinking) water shortages (in parts of our world). As Legrand *et al.* (2017) explain, scarcity of water and numerous instances of bad water management threaten our food supplies and health, ecosystems and biodiversity, and economic development across our globe. For example, in the same period this book was written, Cape Town in South Africa faced an immediate and urgent water crisis. Both as result of a three-year drought and water consumption patterns of local residents and businesses, water was literally running out. Most of us are also familiar with satellite pictures of the Aral Sea between Kazakhstan and Uzbekistan. Once the fourth largest lake in the world, as a result of Soviet irrigation projects it has now been reduced to a few separate small lakes and swamps that together equal less than 10% of its original size. The once thriving local fishing industry is now virtually non-existent, and salinisation and pollution have become huge threats to public health.

At the risk of sounding like a broken record, once again, it is important to note here that the hospitality industry plays a significant role in this problem. Hospitality experiences are often designed and staged in ways that require large quantities of water. This water use can be linked to irrigating that beautiful garden surrounding the castle hotel mentioned earlier but also to laundering bed sheets, towels and banquet linens. If the experience involves providing accommodation, it also involves water used for showering/bathing. If the experience involves thrilling rides in a theme park, just consider the amount of water needed for water coasters.

Luckily, as with energy and waste management, there is actually a wide range of proven solutions that could assist hospitality businesses and professionals in reducing their water use. Legrand et al. (2017) mention quite a few of these solutions, such as maintaining taps, valves and pipes, maintaining and upgrading toilets, installing water-saving showerheads, (re)using greywater, and so on. You could also install dry composting toilets, water-saving washing machines, keep the temperature of the water in the pool a little lower, create gardens with plants that do not need as much water and without fountains and water features. You can also collect rainwater and use it for irrigating the garden and flushing toilets. Finally, as with your carbon footprint, an alternative way to reduce you ultimate water footprint is to offset your direct water use by supporting charities and projects that focus on improving water management in other parts of the world.

Obviously, like with waste, some specific types of water use really are a matter of choice. Just consider the water use involved with wellness centres and facilities offered by a number of hospitality businesses but also the water needed to keep a golf course that is part of a resort located in a (former) desert in perfect playing condition. However, maybe the best example of how reducing your water use is not just a matter of technological solutions or adjusting processes is food. Your direct water use and your ultimate (negative or positive) impact on water management and water scarcity in other parts of the world is very much influenced by choices you make with respect to the food and drinks you serve as part of the hospitality experience you stage.

Food and drinks

In fact, food and drinks are not only an integral part of many hospitality experiences; they are also directly linked to a significant part of the negative environmental (and sometimes social) impact of the hospitality industry.

In his book *Fundamentals of Sustainable Development* (2017), Roorda illustrates this perfectly by referring to the consumption of meat and the way we have organised our food chains to support this. Cattle bred for meat production are usually fed vegetables such as grass, maize and soya. Most of these vegetables used to be grown locally and most farmers would therefore have a mixed farm. However, these days, a number of farmers in countries with high meat production, such as Vietnam and some European countries, actually import most of the animal feed they need from countries such as Brazil. This means that nutrients in the soil of South America are basically transported to Asia and Europe, and end up in the ground there through the manure of the cattle. This leads to high levels of nitrate in water and land, acidification of water and land, and so on. In turn, in South America the lower levels of nutrients in the soil lead to less fertile soil and erosion. Together, this leads to low quality drinking water and acid rain in some parts of our world, and loss of rainforest as a result of having to move agricultural activities to more fertile soil in others. Ecosystems are ruined, biodiversity further decreases, less greenhouse gases are absorbed, and less land is available for farmers in meat-producing countries to grow their own food. However, the list of problems associated with the way we have organised our food chains and our consumption patterns does not stop there. Meat production requires enormous amounts of water. Meat production also leads to methane being released into the air as a result of the gases produced by cattle. Methane is a greenhouse gas that is even more powerful than CO_2, with powerful being a negative thing here because it refers to a higher contribution to climate change. The transporting of animal feed from one part of our world to another and the transporting of the meat to yet other parts of the world obviously also leads to CO_2 emissions and the emissions of other polluting particles. And then, to top it off, the end product that we consume, meat, is actually a very inefficient sources of proteins; one of the nutrients that we, humans, need to survive. Cattle need to eat enormous amounts of vegetable proteins, in the form of animal feed, to create meat with animal proteins. Every kilogram of animal protein requires at least 10 kilograms of vegetable proteins. Through this process, we actually waste a lot of nutrients and we do so while we already use more resources, such as fertile soil, than our Earth can provide in the long run. And then ... we actually waste a significant portion of all food and drinks available to us for consumption. Vegetables and fruit in supermarkets are thrown away as soon as little spots or dents appear. Many of us overestimate the size of our stomachs when preparing our meals or buying take-away lunch, and a lot of the leftovers end up in garbage cans.

Some of us have decided that something needs to change. We buy more biological, organic, seasonal and local produce and products in supermarkets. More and more people have become vegans and vegetarians or at least so-called flexitarians – the latter representing someone who still eats meat occasionally. Others have joined food-sharing initiatives, often by making use of dedicated apps and platforms, such as OLIO in the UK and Too Good To Go, which started in Denmark but is now used in eight European countries. In some of these initiatives, hospitality companies such as restaurants participate through selling their surplus food at a reduced price.

However, it would be fair to say that hospitality businesses and professionals have not yet joined this grassroots movement en masse. Unfortunately, a lot of food and drinks are still wasted; today, up to 50% (!) of the waste stream generated by the hospitality industry is made up of food waste (Legrand *et al.*, 2017). Nearly half of this food waste stems from the food preparation stage but it is also linked to customer returns and, for instance, to using buffets as a means to serve food and drinks to guests and diners, as discussed in Chapter 1. Meanwhile, the menus in most restaurants are still dominated by meat and (unsustainably caught) fish. Food outlets in theme parks in some parts of our world consider a turkey leg to represent *a snack* and entice visitors with an adrenaline rush, from that wild rollercoaster ride they just enjoyed, with messages full of words like 'meat', 'bigger' and 'beast'. At the other extreme, a posh hotel in Amsterdam flies in small plastic bottles of mineral water from South Africa for their guests who have flown in from the States.

Maybe even more so than with respect to energy and water, once again, a lot of the negative impacts associated with these practices come down to choices that are in no way constrained by today's state of technology or having to invest in new equipment or processes. Most kitchens are perfectly equipped to prepare more sustainable food and waste less of it. Local and seasonal produce can be used to prepare meals that are just as flavoursome, if not more flavoursome, than meals using ingredients that have to be flown in from all parts of our globe. Reducing customer returns is not rocket science; again and again, experiments have shown that simply using smaller plates will not only significantly reduce customer returns for buffets but is also perfectly acceptable to customers in à la carte restaurants. Many of them would actually feel more comfortable with smaller portions, both at the moment the meal is served to them and at the moment they (do not) have to send back whatever is left on their plate because they could not possibly eat more than they have already done.

Building (materials and furnishing)

However, in contrast to these choices with respect to the food you serve, some decisions to further sustainability, and the feasibility of specific solutions to do so, can very well be constrained by availability of technologies and/or investments required to make use of them. Most of these are directly linked to the facilities that form the context for staging hospitality experiences. For instance, energy and water use resulting from hospitality operations very much depend on these facilities and thus on decisions made in the design and construction phases of these facilities.

Just consider a hotel located in a monumental/listed building which is poorly insulated, with numerous big windows without double glazing but with stained glass features and a heating system that is based on a huge gas burner that heats water which runs through separate radiators in all hotel rooms. Obviously, the characteristics of this building can make it very difficult to minimise the energy used for operating this hotel. Simultaneously, legal and financial constraints might make it infeasible to renovate the building in such a way that it becomes more energy-efficient. Also, the specific technologies available to at least reduce the ultimate carbon footprint might be limited. For instance, separate radiators are not a good fit with geothermal installations for heating. Typically, these installations only work in combination with low temperature floor heating. You might be able to replace the single-glazed windows with double-glazed windows and even manage to preserve the (appearance of) stained glass features but reducing the size of the windows could be tricky, even if it is an option from a legal perspective, because the huge natural bricks used in constructing the original outside walls are no longer available. Finally, choices made 200 years ago with respect to the materials used in the building and the way it has been constructed make it impossible to avoid significant water and energy use in renovating or deconstructing/demolishing it. In the case of the latter, most materials used in the original building are not suitable for reuse or recycling, which makes the choice to demolish the old building and create a new facility an unattractive one from a sustainable development perspective, especially considering the energy, water and materials required for building a new facility.

Even in circumstances that constraints associated with an existing building do not play a role, not all technologically and financially feasible options can be applied in all of those circumstances. Using wind as an energy source is going to be tricky in regions with a climate that leads to a lot of windless days. Solar panels on the roof of a theatre next to a skyscraper that blocks the sun does not make a lot of sense. Geothermal energy requires drilling holes, which might be difficult if your facility is located on ground that is mostly made up of rocks.

Simultaneously, in almost any situation you can still make a number of choices with respect to what specific energy and other resources you will use and the materials you are going to apply. Some of these decisions relate only to the environmental (and sometimes social) impact of the construction phase, others will significantly influence the impact of the operation phase and beyond. These days, 'circular economy' represents a popular term for this context and it refers to a concept that could assist in the decision-making process. Simply put, creating a circular economy relates to applying materials and products that allow for reuse, repair, refurbishing or recycling once you discard them or that have been created through applying these techniques to existing materials and products. NH Hotels represents an early adapter of this concept. They launched a project in 2011 to collect bottle stoppers in their hotels, which were then transformed into floor and wall coverings for insulation and cladding purposes.

As hip and trendy as the term circular economy might seem and sound, it actually is not really a new concept at all. In essence, it is not that different from the cradle-to-cradle concept launched by McDonough and Braungart in 2002. Martins Hotels in Belgium has applied this concept for quite some time now by using recyclable carpet tiles in their renovated hotels. The tiles are not only produced using recycled textiles but there is also the added benefit of only having to replace damaged tiles in case of wear and tear or stains, instead of having to renew the whole carpet. Before cradle-to-cradle, The Natural Step was the sustainable way to go. Like circular economy and cradle-to-cradle, it revolves around achieving sustainability in the way things are designed, built/constructed and produced through accounting for environmental (and social) consequences of using specific resources and materials. And before The Natural Step, you might ask? Well, we simply referred to these things as reuse, repair and recycling. These terms might not be as sexy but they are as relevant today as back in the day, maybe even more so.

Within the context of designing, building/constructing and furnishing hospitality facilities, Legrand *et al.* (2017) mention a number of other interesting principles, concepts and certification schemes, such as preserving vegetation cover, energy and resource independence, giving consideration to embodied energy, eco-design, life-cycle design, zero-energy buildings, LEED, BREEAM, passive housing, and more. Ultimately, it is irrelevant what specific labels or names you put on specific decisions, technologies and processes. Like with energy, water, waste and food, the combination of these three elements determines the actual impact of buildings and materials used by hospitality companies. Similarly, some of these combinations increase the negative environmental and sometimes social impact, others decrease it. For any given situation, it thus comes down to figuring out what combination would lead to a minimal negative or even positive impact. For almost all situations, there is an abundance of information already *out there* that can assist and inspire hospitality businesses and professionals to pick the best possible combination for their particular situation.

CASE 2.1

Finch Bay Galápagos

Introduction

Finch Bay Galápagos is a boutique hotel with 27 rooms, based on Santa Cruz Island. The hotel has been awarded prizes, and has been a finalist in competitions, several times for its efforts towards sustainability. The hotel calls it 'our commitment to Galápagos'.

What do they do?

As is discussed in this chapter, there are many different technological solutions when it comes to the big five of sustainable hospitality operations: energy, waste, water, food/drinks and building (materials and furnishing). Finch Bay has applied solutions in all of these areas, namely:

- Energy-saving measures (solar panels, LED light bulbs, movement sensors, more efficient electrical appliances), improved insulation, monitoring energy use, drying sheets and linen outdoors instead of using dryers, alternative transportation for employees (bikes);
- Solid waste management programme, recycling programme, biodegradable soap, detergent, and shampoo, homemade compost, refillable water bottles, cleaning public beach daily;
- Water treatment plant, collecting rainwater, watering gardens at coolest time of the day, monitoring water system to avoid leaks;
- Agricultural farm, buying locally, organic products, pesticide and preservative free options;
- Recycled glass was used in paving stones on the island.

Figure 2.1 Finch Bay's chef at work
Courtesy of: Finch Bay Galápagos

So what?

Whilst above-mentioned solutions might seem logical and not necessarily innovative, it needs to be said that the key to Finch Bay's success story lies in their cooperation and communication. Signing up for awards is not only a way for them to get recognition for their efforts, but they also hope it will inspire other hospitality businesses, locally and globally, to do the same. Especially since Finch Bay is the first eco-hotel in Galápagos, they serve as a pioneer in implementing technologies to reduce a hospitality company's environmental impact. Furthermore, Finch Bay is a key stakeholder in projects together with the local government and local NGOs to develop an effective recycling programme.

When traveling to the Galápagos Islands, tourists have already been made aware of the (need for) conservation of the islands. For example, you can only book return flights as a non-resident. Sustainable tourism is key at Galápagos. But Finch Bay takes this one step further by giving guests an eco-friendly welcome speech to encourage pro-environmental behaviour during their stay. Also, when visiting their website, you can already find information on their home page on 'their passion to preserve'. And when reading their information on sustainability, it doesn't only tell you what the hotel does, but also how you, as a guest, can contribute.

Source: Finch Bay, https://www.finchbayhotel.com

Travindy, www.travindy.com

CASE 2.2

Landal Mont Royal

Introduction

Landal Mont Royal, in the German Mosel Valley, is one of the holiday parks of Landal GreenParks. Landal GreenParks has been named in April 2018 as the most sustainable travel supplier by the Sustainable Brand Index. In 2017, their CSR manager was awarded the title 'CSR Manager of the Year' at the National Sustainability Congress in the Netherlands. Their 87 parks are located in nine countries in Europe. On their website (Dutch section only), you can find more information on why they want to be sustainable and engaged.

What do they do?

Landal GreenParks is known for its sustainability efforts, as shown by the awards and recognition mentioned above. The chain of holiday parks claims it wants to be connected to nature, guests and society. In terms of the big five of sustainable hospitality operations, they have applied the following in Landal Mont Royal – which has 99 bungalows of which 74 have recently been redeveloped:

- The 74 bungalows are gas-free and energy neutral. This is realised through solar panels, which guarantee that the bungalows generate at least as much energy as they use in a year. Any surplus energy goes to the 25 existing bungalows in the park. Movement sensors have been installed in halls and toilets and guests can use a *green button* to switch off all power in one go.
- Wooden furniture is used, which is made from recycled teak and oak. In the bedrooms, carpet is used which is made from scrapped fish nets. Any other flooring is also made from recyclable or upcycled material. Overall, 80% of the materials of the old bungalows were reused in the 74 redeveloped ones.

So what?

Together, these efforts could be argued to represent a best practice on choices you can make as a hospitality business. What is interesting to mention though, is that Landal also chose to install saunas and sunbeds in the luxury versions of the redeveloped bungalows. And, as a guest, you can park up to three cars next to these bungalows. This raises the question whether this case represents a best practice or a typical example of how companies that engage in sustainability efforts often struggle to find and follow a clear path.

Source: Duurzaam Ondernemen, www.duurzaam-ondernemen.nl

Landal GreenParks, www.landal.com

That status quo again and how to challenge it

The previous section has reviewed five key topics with respect to making the hotel industry less unsustainable. This review has shown that hospitality businesses and professionals could address all five topics by drawing upon the vast body of knowledge, inspiring best practices, checklists, certification schemes and dedicated initiatives already *out there*. For some aspects of these five key topics, it would definitely help to invest in new technologies, equipment and processes. However, this review has shown that making progress with respect to all of these topics can also be done without complicated technologies and huge investments in new processes and equipment. It often comes down to simply deciding to do things differently, making a choice. There is really no reason why hospitality companies could *not* address all five areas based on a well-thought-out, coherent and ambitious approach that fits with their specific circumstances.

However, in Chapter 1 we have had to conclude that a majority of hospitality companies seem stuck in the efficiency phase of organisational change towards sustainability (Benn *et al.*, 2014) and that sustainability principles have not yet been fully integrated into the core business strategies, tactics and operations of these companies. In this first chapter, we have also highlighted some possible explanations for this status quo and two very good reasons for not accepting it. The second of these two reasons is that the characteristics of the hospitality industry, and the product it offers to customers, actually place it in a perfect position to move well beyond merely reducing its own negative impacts and it could ultimately serve as a catalyst to achieving sustainable development of our societies.

This contrast between *what is* and *what could be*, both with respect to the direct negative impact of this industry and its potential broader role in achieving sustainable development of our societies, underpins the need to have a look at the possible explanations for the status quo in more detail.

One of the possible explanations is that hospitality companies, like any other type of company, need to make a profit to survive in today's highly competitive free market. As Jones *et al.* (2016) explain, the hospitality industry is certainly not the exception in focusing on financial performance and (economic) growth; it is something that can be witnessed in almost all sectors of our global economy, as well as in decision-making by politicians and others that create the constraints for operating within the free market. The fact that applying specific (advanced) technologies and processes to improve sustainability performance can come at the cost of short-term financial performance, because they require substantial investments, consequently acts as a barrier to adopting them in many sectors of our economy.

Simultaneously, it would probably be fair to say that the hospitality industry is not (yet) a frontrunner when it comes to adopting sustainable technologies and processes. In fact, it is regularly described as somewhat of a laggard in this respect. This is where the specific characteristics of the hospitality industry, and how it differs from most other industries, come in. As indicated in Chapter 1, this industry encompasses a wide range of different types of businesses, ranging from small independent businesses to powerful and globally operating chains. Many of those small businesses simply cannot afford expensive technologies and processes. Unfortunately, oftentimes they also lack the knowledge and time to look for (less expensive) alternatives or, at least, that is how they see it themselves. These small businesses, operated by hospitality professionals (and oftentimes their families) who consider themselves as not having the means to tackle such a gigantic problem as sustainable development, make up a significant portion of the hospitality industry.

However, another significant portion of this industry consists of those big (international) chains. Surely, a company like Marriott does have the (financial) means and expertise to pick the best possible combination of decisions, technologies and processes for *their* hotels? Well, as it turns out, the situation in practice is quite a bit more complicated than that. These complications are linked to particular (developments in) ownership constructions that are typical for this industry. For instance, for more and more hotels and restaurants the owner of the building/facility that serves as the context for staging hospitality experiences for guests and diners is actually not the same person or party as the one who is responsible for staging those experiences. In fact, oftentimes there are many different stakeholders involved in the ownership and operation of such a hospitality company, such as the owner of the building, the owner of the land on which the building is located, the person or party who is entitled to the company's profits, the person or party running and managing the company (on a daily basis) and the owner of the brand (name) displayed on the outside wall of the building (Melissen *et al.*, 2016). The specific responsibilities, obligations and authority of all people and parties involved in these arrangements have usually been laid down in (painstaking) detail in so-called management contracts and franchise agreements that are 'firmly positioned in the "control and manage paradigm"' (Melissen *et al.*, 2016, p. 39).

Obviously, this really complicates matters when it comes to improving sustainability performance of an individual establishment. Those contracts usually make it virtually impossible for one of the parties involved to simply *decide to do things differently from now on*. Renovating the building could be interesting from a sustainability perspective but who is going to pick up the bill? Oftentimes, these buildings are actually owned by (real estate) investment firms. People whose salaries and bonuses depend on maximising dividends for the firm's shareholders through renting out, buying and selling real estate are the ones managing these firms. Chances of them favouring significant investments in upgrading these buildings, from a sustainable development perspective, are usually rather slim. The actual operator of the building usually works based on a management contract stipulating that their fee for doing so depends on yearly revenues and gross operating profit. As indicated earlier, investments in sustainable technologies and equipment might thus hurt them financially. Another possible complication relates to possible detachment of particular stakeholders involved in the ownership and operation of a particular establishment in relation to the actual local business and its environment, both geographically and mentally. The headquarters of the company responsible for operating a local business, such as a hotel or a restaurant, might very well be located on the other side of the globe. This might make it rather difficult for them to account for 'the interests of and impacts on local socio-economic and environmental systems in decision-making or, at least, make it more difficult to actually involve local stakeholders' (Melissen *et al.*, 2016, p. 40).

Similarly, companies in all sectors still find it difficult to convince (potential) customers to pick sustainable products and services over unsustainable ones, especially if that means paying more for them. However, the specific characteristics of hospitality companies, or rather the characteristics of the ultimate product they offer to their customer and the way in which they do so, might very well explain why this industry is (still) relatively unsustainable. As indicated in Chapter 1, many hospitality professionals are convinced that their customers want to be oversupplied, prefer luxurious experiences, and like to be seduced and excited based on escaping reality. To be fair, we, in our roles as guests, diners and visitors, have given them plenty of reasons to assume so, for instance based on our loyalty to companies and experiences that can really not be described in any other way than being unsustainable and our tendency to use more energy/water and produce more waste away from home. We will return to the questions of whether this assumption is correct and whether it really has to function as a barrier to promoting sustainable products, services, experiences and behaviours in the next chapter. Here, it is important to note that, once again, the specific characteristics of the hospitality industry, and its core product, seem to play a role in explaining the status quo with respect to (further) reducing its negative impacts from a sustainable development perspective.

Interestingly, the train of thought presented in this section suggests that the very same characteristics identified in Chapter 1 as reasons why the hospitality industry could serve as a catalyst for achieving sustainable development of wider society also (still) serve as barriers for changing the status quo with respect to its direct negative impacts. The fact that those involved with individual hospitality establishments often represent influential globally operating companies not only makes them powerful allies in promoting sustainable development but also brings with it the complications involved with the ownership constructions that characterise this industry. On the one hand, the local businesses that together shape this industry might be intertwined with local and regional social, economic and environmental systems, and thus represent *natural* partners and stakeholders in sustainable development of these systems. On the other, actual decisions made by these businesses might very well be made by persons and parties with geographical and mental detachment from this particular establishment and its direct environment, and ultimate decision-making might very well be constrained by contracts and agreements that can only be described as not being conducive to sustainable development (Melissen *et al.*, 2016). Or, in contrast, these decisions need to be made by professionals, and oftentimes also their families, who consider themselves to not be equipped, both financially and in terms of knowledge and time, to make any significant contribution to achieving sustainable development. And then there is the core product, i.e., hospitality experiences. Pleasant, enjoyable experiences that make you happy could create the perfect circumstances to discuss sustainability and to experience that sustainability can be fun, rewarding and not necessarily more expensive. Ironically, the very experiences currently staged by this industry that create those favourable circumstances are mostly based on principles that can only be described as contradictory to sustainability principles.

There we have it: two sides of the same coin. Is the hospitality industry the villain or the hero, or both? Maybe it is simply a matter of choice. As this chapter has shown, pursuing sustainable development need not be complicated. It does not always require huge investments. Sometimes it simply requires making different decisions, deciding to do things differently. As worded so eloquently by Parrish, 'there is growing anticipation that it is not human technology so much as patterns of human activity that are challenging the sustainability of human development' (2007, p. 846). Therefore, maybe the best way to change the status quo is not to focus on technology but on people. The authors of this book certainly think so and therefore the next chapter looks at why people behave the way they do in more detail. Subsequent chapters than apply these lessons to show how hospitality businesses and professionals could apply them and how the villain could become the hero.

SUMMARY

Based on reading this chapter, we hope you will understand and remember the following:

- Five elements that are responsible for a significant part of the negative impact of the hospitality industry, are:

  o energy;
  o waste;
  o water;
  o food and drinks;
  o the building (including materials and furnishing).

- Energy use for typical hospitality facilities is higher compared to other types of buildings, leading to a high carbon footprint.

- Two key areas to reduce the hospitality industry's carbon footprint, are:
  - using renewable instead of non-renewable energy sources;
  - reducing the overall amount of energy used.
- Examples of renewable energy sources are wind, solar or hydro power, and these could also come from local suppliers.
- Reducing the amount of energy needed can be done through, for example, insulation, window sizes and materials used for walls and roofs.
- Waste generated in the hospitality industry can be divided into two categories:
  - wet or organic waste;
  - dry waste (plastic, glass, paper, e-waste).
- Recycling or re-using materials is not always common practice (yet) in the hospitality industry.
- The best solution for waste is to make different choices, e.g., using recycled materials or not putting a TV in the room.
- There are quite a few technological solutions for water use, e.g., (re)using greywater and dry composting toilets.
- Meat production requires enormous amounts of water, and produces a lot of greenhouse gas emissions.
- Half of the waste stream from hospitality is food waste. Half of the food waste stems from food preparation.
- Choices such as reducing portion size could help reduce food waste.
- Circular economy builds on concepts such as cradle-to-cradle and The Natural Step. All of them revolve around recycling, repairing and reusing materials.
- The very same reasons why the hospitality industry could serve as a catalyst for achieving sustainable development now seem to act as barriers for moving to the next level.
- Resolving this situation might not require huge investments or complicated technologies but rather making different choices and focusing on people's decisions and behaviours.

FOOD FOR THOUGHT

Based on the content of this chapter, the following questions, challenges and topics could serve as interesting starting points for further discussion:

- If you were the decision-maker in a hospitality business, would you invest in improving technologies and processes or in changing human behaviour?
- How do you perceive your own behaviour when taking the 'Big Five' of this chapter into account? And do you see a difference in your behaviour compared to people close to you?
- What are the pros and cons of carbon offsetting?

References

Benn, S., Dunphy, D. & Griffiths, A. (2014). *Organizational change for corporate sustainability* (3rd ed.) New York: Routledge.

Geyer, R., Jambeck, J.R. & Law, K. (2017). 'Production, use, and fate of all plastics ever made'. *Science Advances*, 3(7), e1700782.

Jones, P., Hillier, D. & Comfort, D. (2016). 'Sustainability in the hospitality industry: Some personal reflections on corporate challenges and research agendas'. *International Journal of Contemporary Hospitality Management*, 28 (1), 36–67.

Legrand, W., Sloan, P. & Chen, J.S. (2017). *Sustainability in the hospitality industry: Principles of sustainable operations* (3rd ed.) London: Routledge.

Melissen, F., van Ginneken, R. & Wood, R. C. (2016). 'Sustainability challenges and opportunities arising from the owner-operator split in hotels'. *International Journal of Hospitality Management*, 54, 35–42.

Parrish, B.D. (2007). 'Designing the sustainable enterprise'. *Futures*, 39(7), 846–860.

Roorda, N. (2017). *Fundamentals of sustainable development* (2nd ed.). New York: Routledge.

CHAPTER
3 People and sustainability

Introduction

The previous chapter concluded with highlighting the crucial role of people in achieving sustainable development, also, and maybe even especially, with respect to the hospitality industry. Therefore, this chapter explores the impact of contexts shaped by this industry on people's decisions and behaviours. In order to understand this impact, it is important to first understand the basics of human decision-making and human behaviour. Therefore, the subsequent sections are devoted to reviewing these basics from two perspectives: (1) how do they explain the unsustainable course our societies are on, and (2) how could the same logic be used to create contexts that stimulate sustainable decisions and behaviour? The final section then provides a first exploration of how this logic could be applied in the hospitality industry to assist in changing the status quo discussed in the previous chapters.

Human behaviour and unsustainability

The suggestion in the final section of the previous chapter that those aiming to contribute to achieving sustainable development should focus on people instead of technology may have come across as a bold statement. It is not. We, the authors, are neither the first nor the only ones making this suggestion. In fact, over the years, a growing number of researchers, practitioners, politicians and activists have put forward similar claims. For instance, in 1973, Maloney and Ward already stated that the solution for sustainability problems would have to come from insights with respect to (changing) human behaviour. Their paper was preceded and followed by two of the most authoritative and influential publications regarding the link between human behaviour and (un)sustainability: Garrett Hardin's 1968 paper entitled 'Tragedy of the Commons' and Robyn Dawes' paper, 'Social Dilemmas', in 1980. The tragedy of the commons actually represents a specific type of social dilemma and social dilemmas play a crucial role in explaining our tendency, as human beings, to engage in unsustainable behaviour. Unfortunately, resolving these dilemmas is anything but a sinecure. This section explains why.

The complexities of human behaviour

A number of theories on human behaviour are in some way or another based on two main concepts: (1) expectations; and (2) value. These so-called expectancy-value models suggest that we, humans, are more likely to engage in specific behaviour if we expect that behaviour to result in an outcome that we value. They suggest that we *calculate* or *compute* the expected utility of all behavioural alternatives linked to a specific decision before making that decision. Those expected utilities are calculated through multiplying the likelihood of all possible outcomes for a particular behavioural alternative with the respective values we attach to those outcomes, and then adding all resulting scores. The behavioural alternative with the highest expected utility score is the one we will pick.

Despite the continued popularity of these models in psychology, but also in other fields, by now some serious doubts have been raised about the actual predictive value of these models in real-life situations. For one, because it is probably unreasonable to assume that we, people living our daily lives, actually base all our choices on calculating or computing various probabilities, values and ultimate scores based on multiplying and adding them. If we really did this, we could probably only make a few dozen decisions each day, while in reality we make thousands and thousands of decisions each day. Just consider the first few minutes of a typical working day. Your alarm goes off. You then either press the snooze or the stop button. You do this with your right or your left hand – or another body part of your choice, should you so desire. In the case that you have chosen to press the stop button, you either decide to actually get out of bed or you do not. In the case that you actually get out of bed, you decide on whether you will take a shower or a bath. You decide on which towel you will use for drying yourself afterwards before you step into the bathtub, because you need to hang it close to the bathtub before you get the tap running and step in, otherwise the whole bathroom floor will get wet at a later stage. By the way, will you start the tap running with your right or you left hand, or …? Will you step into the bathtub with your left leg first, your right leg, or will you just jump in? And so on. By now, you have already made dozens of decisions and it has literally only been minutes since the alarm went off. In other words, as logical as expectancy-value calculations may seem, it is clearly not something we actually do for most decisions we make.

Probably the most famous and widely used theories on human behaviour to date are the theory of reasoned action (Fishbein and Ajzen, 1975) and the theory of planned behaviour (Ajzen, 1985; Ajzen and Madden, 1986). In both theories, your attitude towards a particular behaviour constitutes a crucial element of the likelihood you will engage in that behaviour. Interestingly, this attitude concept is very much based on the same logic as expectancy-value thinking. Not surprisingly, therefore, these theories have also been widely criticised for not being complete or applicable to practical situations. It is beyond the scope of this book to explain all details of these discussions. However, it is important to note here that more and more researchers have come to the conclusion that, while these theories may have been influential and helpful in furthering our understanding of human behaviour over the years, their usefulness for predicting and influencing real-life behaviours, especially within the context of (un)sustainability, is actually rather limited.

To illustrate this, consider the simple fact that more and more people these days are quite worried about the current unsustainable course of our societies and would like this situation to be resolved. In fact, it would probably be hard to find anyone that would prefer the predictions of the Club of Rome, as discussed in Chapter 1, to become reality over us finding a way to prevent further climate change and make poverty disappear. In other words, most of us subscribe to the values that the concept of sustainable development represents and have a positive attitude towards achieving it. However, most of us also still engage in behaviours that contribute to the opposite; that can only be described as unsustainable. Apparently, especially when it comes to behaviours that are relevant to sustainable development, our decisions and behaviours are pretty complex. Or rather, predicting and influencing our decisions and behaviours is more complicated than these popular theories and models suggest. Simultaneously though, numerous public campaigns and policies today, that have purposely and specifically been set up and installed to promote sustainability, are still based on assumptions founded in the very same logic that these theories and models are based on. We will return to this issue later in this chapter but, obviously, this is probably part of the explanation for the limited success of these policies and campaigns.

Our tragedy of the commons and our social dilemmas

To truly understand the complexities involved with unsustainable behaviour, it helps to take a step back from the complicated chemistry and calculations involved with trying to grasp issues such as climate change, and focus on the essence of what is actually happening with our planet and us, humans, who live our lives by using the resources it offers.

The 'tragedy of the commons' is a concept that can assist us in doing so (Hardin, 1968). Hardin uses the example of a piece of grassland, used by multiple herdsmen, to illustrate this concept. Obviously, each herdsman tries to provide for his family the best way he can. This implies that each herdsman is faced with the question of whether it would be beneficial to him and his family to add another animal to his herd. An extra animal would mean extra income through being able to sell more milk and/or meat. Simultaneously, an extra animal would also mean that less grass is available per animal for all animals of all herdsmen that use the same piece of grassland. However, from the perspective of an individual herdsman this

possible negative consequence is clearly outweighed by the positive consequences of adding an extra animal to his herd because the negative
consequences are spread out over all herdsmen, whereas all extra income
goes directly to him. Unfortunately, if all herdsmen reason like that, they
will all add an extra animal to their respective herds. Maybe even more
than one. The number of animals grazing the grassland will therefore
increase significantly, whereas the grassland itself and the amount of grass
it can provide stay the same. Actually, the latter is probably not true
because overgrazing will likely degrade the grassland and probably sooner
than later the grassland will not be enough to feed all animals, animals will
die and the herdsmen will be left with no income. In other words, what
seemed like a perfectly reasonable course of action for individual herdsmen,
will actually lead to tragedy for all of them.

Obviously, this tragedy represents a simplified version of what is happening to
our planet. It illustrates how overpopulating our planet and overusing its
resources will cause, and has already caused, serious problems for all of us. It
also illustrates how all of this seems to be happening while most of us tell
ourselves that we are not to blame because we have to make the decisions we
make and we have to behave the way we do to meet our needs and those of the
people close to us. Through making these decisions, we are actually doing exactly
what we are *supposed to do* from the perspective of a capitalistic economic system
based on free markets. This system dominates most of our societies when it comes
to setting the rules for interactions between businesses and consumers, how
professionals in those businesses are *supposed to act*, and the decisions we expect
from politicians and policy-makers. We have come to rely on this system for the
way in which we fulfil many of our needs and wishes. Interestingly, or maybe
ironically, the logic on which this system is based very much contradicts the logic
used by Hardin to explain the tragedy of the commons.

Ultimately, mechanisms incorporated in the free market system can be
traced back to the train of thought presented by Adam Smith in *The Wealth
of Nations* (1776). Smith is commonly acknowledged as the one laying the
foundations for economic theory and the spiritual father of the socio-
economic system that creates the context for most of our everyday lives.
This train of thought can be summarised as the firm belief that (the
mechanisms incorporated in) free market economies ensure that people
acting in self-interest, for instance by focusing on their own private profit,
material wealth and property, automatically contribute to more prosperity
for all. And, to some extent, it is quite obvious that doing so has actually
benefitted most of us. It would be hard to argue with the fact that this
economic system has helped us to exploit Earth's resources in ways that
have resulted in economic growth, more material wealth for many of us,
better health care for many us, better education for many of us and more
opportunities for many of us, compared to a few hundred years ago, or even
compared to a few decades ago. For many of us this system seems to work!

Not for everybody though, because this same socio-economic system has also created more significant differences between rich and poor, and this same system has not been able to prevent many people across our globe (still) living their lives in poverty, (still) not having access to proper health care, (still) not having access to good education, (still) not having the opportunities that we, privileged ones, living in rich parts of the world, have. What is more, (economic) prosperity for many of us has come at another price. In our pursuit of economic growth and more material wealth, we have become so good at extracting Earth's resources to satisfy our needs that this might very well result in destroying our planet and ourselves. Following Smith's advice has been good to many of us but at the expense of falling into the very trap that Hardin has warned us about. In fact, as indicated earlier, more and more of us are actually quite aware of this. We know we are digging our own hole by basing most of our decisions and behaviours on Smith's logic and ignoring Hardin's warning. Somehow though, we seem reluctant or maybe even unable to stop doing this.

That is *our* tragedy of the commons. Humanity's tragedy represents a particular type of a so-called social dilemma (Dawes, 1980). Simply put, a social dilemma is a situation in which it appears to pay off for each of us, individually, to focus on our own (short-term) interests in our decisions and behaviours but all of us would actually be (much) better off, especially in the long run, if we would all base our decisions and behaviours on the common good. A typical example would be flying. Most of us know perfectly well that to avoid climate change, and all associated catastrophes, it would be best if all of us stopped using airplanes, at least until we have found a way to make flying carbon neutral. However, in practice, most of us still decide to book holidays to tropical islands or long weekend trips to vibrant cities that require us to travel by airplane. Similarly, many of us are fully aware of all environmental and social problems associated with consuming high quantities of meat but does that stop us doing so? No.

One could argue that we have been conditioned by our socio-economic system based on the values of free market capitalism to keep making the decisions we have always made and to keep behaving as we have always behaved. It is just how things work in our world. It is what *everybody* does and it is what has brought us so much. It is how we have arranged our world to satisfy our needs. This system's apparent success, in terms of bringing many of us prosperity, makes it hard to imagine another system replacing it. Communism has proven not to represent a viable alternative. Dictatorships and authoritarianism are simply unacceptable. Basically, free market capitalism is the only system most of us have known and the only system we can imagine being able to satisfy our needs. Adam Smith's logic has transformed into something like a natural law in the minds of many of us; for some, especially politicians, it has even turned into something like a religion. No wonder most of us seem to find it perfectly normal and acceptable to continue booking airplane tickets, eating meat, driving our cars, and so on.

Bring in the Flintstones

However, the conditioning effect of the socio-economic system that has been in place for the last few hundred years is probably not the only possible explanation for our tendency, as a species, to persist in making unsustainable decisions and engaging in unsustainable behaviours. To understand some of our decisions and behaviours today, it might also help to account for the evolutionary bases of our behaviours. Over the course of (human) history, natural selection has not only determined what we look like today but also some of our behavioural tendencies. To illustrate the sustained – pun intended – present-day effect of this process, just consider children's preference for sweets over vegetables. The reason for this is not that parents set out to teach their little ones to pick sugar over vegetable proteins. Children have this natural tendency to like sugary things because their brains have been programmed that way by evolution. In days long gone, when we still roamed on plains of an 'uncivilised' planet, you could not simply walk into a supermarket to buy your food; you had to hunt for it, search for it, and you would be doing so in an environment that was anything but convenient and safe. Therefore, ripe fruit would be something you would never pass on because it provided you with much-needed calories to survive. This preference to go for ripe over unripe, for sweet over not sweet, is thus something that comes natural to us. It is something we have inherited from our ancestors.

In their paper dedicated to this topic, Griskevicius *et al.* (2012) highlight five of these tendencies and how they explain our self-destructive behaviour from a sustainable development perspective. The first is our propensity for self-interest. Natural selection has taught us to care about the replication of our own genes, even if this comes at the expense of the survival of the genes of strangers. This explains that our instinct tells us, even today, to focus on our self-interest and that of our loved ones instead of the interests of strangers in many of the day-to-day decisions we make. Obviously, this tendency is closely linked to, and partially explains, our predisposition to focus on self-interest instead of the common good in social dilemma situations. In fact, the tragedy of the commons concept perfectly captures this tendency in situations in which we decide to behave unsustainably because it serves our own (short-term) interests. This also explains why public campaigns that promote sustainable behaviour through urging people to put the interest of humanity in the long term over their own short-term interests often prove ineffective.

The second tendency identified by Griskevicius *et al.* is linked to our desire for relative status. This desire stems from the fact that those considered successful by others have the best chance to *seduce* the other sex to *reproduce*, and thus guarantee the survival of their genes. To be honest, this was not just the case in the old days; it is still true today. No wonder we are prone to (excessive) consumption of luxurious products, services and experiences, and accumulating and showing off our material wealth.

Third, we instinctively copy the behaviour of others. In the dangerous and uncertain circumstances of the old days, it was not good advice to learn how to survive based on trial-and-error. In fact, only those who were smart enough to mimic the behaviour of older and successful people, who obviously knew exactly how to survive, would stand a chance of surviving themselves. This desire still plays a crucial role today and explains why people, for instance, find it difficult to motivate themselves to throw their own waste in trash bins at a parking site along a highway if that site is littered with trash.

The final two tendencies mentioned by Griskevicius *et al.* are our predisposition to be short-sighted and our proneness to disregard impalpable concerns. Similar to copying others' behaviours, these tendencies are linked to the uncertainties of surviving in the old days. Thinking about the future was not a luxury you could afford; you had to focus on the right here and right now. Concentrating on what you could actually see, feel, touch, hear or smell supported this. If and when you felt hungry, you had better start hunting or gathering. If and when you smelt fire, you had better run. Together, these two tendencies explain why many of us manage to live our lives the way we do and make the decisions we make, also those that harm the environment and aggravate climate change, without feeling alarmed all the time about the unsustainable course our societies are on. We simply have not been programmed *properly* to react *appropriately* to problems that evolve as slowly as climate change. Our brain is not designed to perceive and detect dangers that are less obvious and tangible, such as pollution. As long as 'our house smells just fine, our neighbourhood has trees, our water tastes fine, and our food supply at the store is plentiful' (Griskevicius *et al.*, 2012, p. 124), we find it difficult to really register unsustainability. We might understand the basics of what is happening but evolution has not (yet) taught us to respond to this in the *right* way.

Promoting sustainable behaviour

All this leaves us in a bit of a pickle, to put it mildly. We, humans, are really good at exploiting Earth's resources to satisfy our (immediate) needs and wishes, and we are really bad at registering the negative consequences, as well as adjusting our behaviour in order to avoid these consequences. Does this mean we are doomed? Have we been programmed to create our own downfall and is it therefore inevitable? Luckily, the answer to these questions is no, or, at least, not necessarily. As Griskevicius *et al.* (2012, p. 116) point out, in reference to Dawkins (1976), 'although our genes are selfish at the ultimate level, selfish genes can and do build organisms that are capable of behaving in ways that are kind, charitable, and sustainable'.

This section explores how the very same lessons learnt and discussed in the previous section could also be used to (purposely) promote sustainable decisions and behaviours. We, humans, might be stubborn, and our decision-making and behaviour might be complex, but we are also pretty predictable and consistent. Apparently, our brains have not really changed that much over the years and chances are that they will not change significantly over the next few decades. Therefore, whilst our mission might be difficult, it is not impossible, because we can draw upon quite a lot of reliable information about what we *do* respond to, what we *do* like and what we *are* inclined to do, today, tomorrow and the day after tomorrow.

Focus on what we do know

In the sciences that deal with human behaviour, such as psychology, the expectancy-value approach and theories such as the theory of planned behaviour still play an important role. They are often used as the starting point for trying to understand, predict and find ways to influence real-life behaviour, also with respect to behaviour relevant to achieving sustainable development. And, to be fair, over the years, this has actually resulted in significant progress with respect to identifying several additional factors and/or determinants that seem to influence sustainability behaviour. Even though we might not know all relevant factors and/or determinants for all particular behaviours and circumstances (yet), we have been able to pinpoint some key areas. For instance, it is now perfectly clear that in our roles as consumers but oftentimes also in our roles as employees, neighbours, voters and professionals, we do *not* rely on actually *computing* expected utility for many of the decisions we make and many of the behaviours we engage in. In our day-to-day lives, habits and routines, as well as unconscious decisions, play a crucial role. We almost automatically buy the same products we have always bought; we display the same behaviours we have always displayed. When we buy that ice cream we really like, we usually do not consider the environmental and social consequences associated with the cocoa beans used for the chocolate in the ice cream. When we prepare dinner, we usually do not consciously prepare more than our family is likely to eat that day. We do not make a detailed calculation based on measuring the calories our spouse and children have already burnt that day. Much more likely, we actually think about very different things when doing so. We prepare the same amount of food as we always do and think about which movie it would be nice to watch that evening while eating. We buy that ice cream because it is a hot day and that is what is on our mind.

Therefore, those who try to influence us in making more sustainable decisions and displaying more sustainable behaviour need to account for this. They need to grab our attention. They also need to be honest and open about what they are trying to do and why they are doing it, especially companies whose products, services and experiences we consume. As discussed in

Chapter 1, by now, we have heard it all before and many of us have become quite sceptical regarding the motives of those claiming to offer us more sustainable products, services and experiences. If you, as a company, make particular claims with respect to the sustainability level of your products, services, processes and actions, you better make sure you can back up those claims. Just displaying a logo on the packaging of your products or a nice plaque next to your front door is not enough. Chances are, we will not even notice them.

In trying to influence us, you also better account for the fact that we all have our own preferences, priorities and values when it comes to sustainability. Some of us feel that climate change is the most important and urgent challenge to address; others trust that this issue will be resolved through technological advancements and would rather have the focus on reducing inequality and eradicating poverty in our world. You might very well find out that we even disagree on these things within our own families, so you must make sure to not address us as if we are all *the same*. Allow and stimulate us to link what you want us to buy or do to what we value (most).

Mind the different values

In fact, if and when promoting sustainable decisions and behaviour, those who do so need to realise that for most people sustainability relates to potential conflicts between their various values. As Steg *et al.* (2014) explain, goal framing theory suggests that, in many situations we face, three different types of goals seem to play a role in what we decide and do: hedonic goals, gain goals and normative goals. Hedonic goals relate to our feelings and lead us to prefer options that make us feel better, such as through avoiding effort, and seeking pleasure and excitement. Gain goals link to our personal resources and stimulate us to protect or increase these resources, such as money and status. Finally, normative goals tell us what would be the *right* thing to do; what would be the appropriate course of action, for instance from an ethical perspective. You could almost say that in any given situation, these three goals are *shouting* for our attention and the one that is triggered the most by a particular situation will likely *win* and determine what we will decide or do.

Obviously, not all of these goals are directly linked to decisions and behaviours that are highly relevant from a sustainable development perspective, or, at least, not to the same extent. What is more, they are oftentimes also in conflict with each other in these situations. Just consider turning down the thermostat in your house. This could save you money and it would be the sustainable thing to do, but it also means the house could feel chilly and that you would have to go upstairs and get a sweater to compensate for that. The same goes for taking the bike to work or school: cheaper and better for the environment but certainly not as pleasant when it is raining and a cold wind is in your face.

In trying to promote sustainable decisions and behaviour, you could account for these goals by purposely trying to resolve some of these conflicts. For instance, you could make sustainable alternatives more fun and less expensive. If the sustainable alternative is just as much fun and not more expensive than the unsustainable alternative, or even more fun and cheaper, there is every chance you could convince people to try it, especially if you manage to get their attention by pointing out these *new* features of this product, service or experience. For some sustainability aspects, this is definitely possible. For instance, local and seasonal food can be just as tasty and less expensive than a meal that is prepared using produce flown in from across the globe.

Another option to navigate the potential conflicts, between the three types of goals we pursue, is to purposely strengthen (the impact of) one of them, like, for instance, the normative goals that favour sustainable decisions and behaviours. You could do this by creating an environment that incorporates specific cues and stimuli linked to these goals. For one, you could make sure that the environment in which you want people to make sustainable decisions or engage in sustainable behaviour contains lots of plants, and pictures of beautiful landscapes and animals, because research has shown that being exposed to *nature* could tap into our so-called dormant biophilia (Griskevicius *et al.*, 2012): the fact that evolution has endowed us with an appreciation and desire for the natural world (Wilson, 2006). In other words, exposure to natural environments, or objects and pictures that resemble a natural environment, could very well strengthen the normative goal that most of us have in common, i.e., to protect that same environment, and thus influence us to make sustainable decisions and display sustainable behaviour.

Combine approaches

All this means that we, humans, might be stubborn and creatures of habit, but we actually are open to changing our routines and trying new things, including sustainable products, services, experiences and behaviour, as long as we are *seduced* to do so by ticking all the right boxes. Sometimes, all that is required is reinforcing our normative goals that already favour sustainable decisions and behaviour; at other times, we need things to be made easier, cheaper or more fun. It is important to strike the right balance in combining these approaches though. For instance, as a company it would not be wise to focus only on hedonic and gain goals in promoting your sustainable products, services and experiences. This would 'make these goals more influential in [future] decision-making [by consumers], thereby weakening normative goals' (Steg *et al.*, 2014, p. 106). If normative goals were ignored, this would make it difficult to make an appeal to them in your future offerings to those same consumers. By then, these consumers would assume you, as a company, do not care about these goals, because you have focused exclusively on the fun and price level of your sustainable products, services and experiences in your interactions with them up to that point. This will make them associate those products, services and experiences with fun and price, and it will also make them see you as a company that only cares about fun and money. Suddenly changing your tactics to focusing on your environmental and social impact, as a company, will probably no longer be seen as being open and honest about your motives, thus result in you running the risk of alienating your customers or, at least, making them sceptical. Obviously, this is not going to help your future efforts with respect to reducing your negative impacts or having a positive impact through involving your customers.

In other words, convincing customers to accept or even prefer sustainable alternatives to unsustainable ones is not impossible, but it still represents a challenge that requires a well thought-out and balanced approach. In fact, you could argue that it usually needs to be based on combining three approaches (Hall, 2013):

1. A utilitarian approach, which aims at providing people with honest and detailed information about the sustainability aspects involved in what you want them to buy or do.
2. A social/psychological approach, which accounts for the fact that solely providing information is usually not enough to convince people, and thus also focuses on the context for these choices and behaviours.
3. A so-called system of provision approach, which also focuses on that context but on a more structural or fundamental level.

At first glance, the second and third approach might seem rather similar, but they really are not. Both try to influence the context for decisions and behaviour, thus promoting sustainability, but whereas the second explicitly focuses on *nudging* people in the *right* direction without limiting their options, the third actually focuses on trying to change the 'institutions, norms, rules, structures and infrastructures that constrain individual decision-making, consumption and lifestyle and social practices' (Hall, 2013, p. 1099).

Nudging people (Thaler and Sunstein, 2008) has become a popular way of trying to promote sustainability, especially amongst policy-makers. A typical example would be to provide people with feedback on their own water and energy use, and that of their neighbours. It taps into our tendency to compare our own behaviour to that of others. If our neighbours use less water and energy, there is every chance that we will try to reduce our own water and energy use because we do not want to be the *laggard* or the *outsider*. Tapping into our dormant biophilia would be another typical example of nudging through changing the (psychical) context for our decisions and behaviour.

Changing the system of provision moves beyond nudging and trying to *seduce* people to make different choices; simply put, this approach suggests that this is not enough or, at least, too slow from a sustainable development perspective, and that for some decisions or behaviours the *logical* and *right* thing to do would be to limit people's options. The most effective way to ensure that people do not engage in unsustainable behaviour is to make it impossible. For instance, if you want to improve air quality in city centres, you could encourage people to take their bikes or use public transport, but you could also simply ban cars from that area. If you want farmers to use fewer pesticides, you could explain to them that it would be better for the environment to use sustainable alternatives (approach 1) or inform them about the great results that other farmers have had with using those sustainable alternatives (approach 2). However, if the negative effects of those pesticides is significant, and farmers are proving reluctant to switch, it might very well be wise to simply make the production, selling and use of those damaging substances illegal (approach 3).

However, this third approach could also be applied at a *lower* level and need not be restricted to actions by policy-makers and authorities. If an individual company wants to promote local, organic and seasonal food, there is no reason why it could not move beyond promoting this to their customers; a restaurant could very well decide to only use this type of produce for preparing the meals they offer to diners. Why would a theme park *have to* sell both fair-trade and non-fair-trade coffee and chocolate to its visitors? We will return to the options available to hospitality businesses and professionals in the final section of this chapter but here it is important to note that, also for (commercial) companies, all three approaches could prove useful in promoting sustainable decisions and behaviour by customers.

CASE 3.1

Ecomama

Introduction

Ecomama calls itself a 'green, quirky and conscious boutique' hostel. Located in Amsterdam, in a former travel agency, the hostel is furnished and decorated with vintage furniture and eco-conscious design.

What does Ecomama do to stimulate pro-environmental behaviour?

Most of the materials in the building are second-hand, or as they call it, vintage. For example, the reception desk is built out of second-hand books. This immediately helps the guest to understand the concept of this hostel. Their employees also explain the hostel's recycling program upon check-in. The hostel's whole value proposition revolves around responsibility and being conscious, although this is done in a humorous, light-hearted and non-pushy way. Consequently, they manage to really make you *feel* it is better to be eco-friendly; they manage to get *under your skin*. For example, they do not tell you to save energy; they send this message through their light switches, which have drawings around them of a hamster-wheel to remind guests of the fact that electricity requires energy.

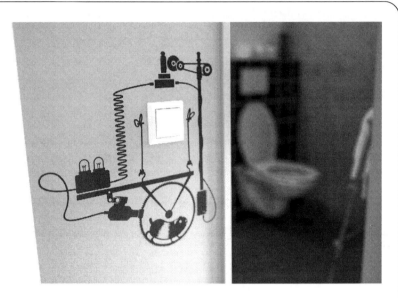

Figure 3.1 The hamster wheel at Ecomama
Courtesy of: Ecomama

So what?

Ecomama is a prime example of just doing it, without overthinking it but still projecting a coherent identity. Sustainability is in their DNA and not forced upon the guest; it is just . . . there. From the moment of visiting their website, up to and including your actual stay, the theme of being sustainable is everywhere: in their communication, their behaviour, their building, their materials and more.

Source: Ecomama (n.d.)

Tap into our Stone Age brain

In combining these three approaches, and linking to the different types of values of people, it could also help to realise that the five evolutionary tendencies discussed earlier not only explain unsustainable decisions and behaviour; they can also be used to promote sustainable alternatives.

Griskevicius *et al.* (2012) illustrate this by referring to the same example they use to explain the sustained effect of our Stone Age brain on our present-day lives. If we acknowledge that our brain has been programmed to prefer sweets to vegetables, what better way to seduce us to eat more vegetables than to sweeten those vegetables? Have you ever wondered why most salad dressings have a sweet flavour? Dressings are the perfect way to make something healthy taste sweet and fatty; exactly what we, humans, have been programmed to like.

In their paper, Griskevicius *et al.* (2012) illustrate that the same reverse logic could be applied to all five evolutionary tendencies discussed earlier. Our propensity for self-interest could be used in messages aimed at using less energy and water. Instead of focusing on the common good, these messages could focus on the negative impacts of using too much energy and water on the lives of the children and grandchildren of the people that need to be convinced. In the old days, we tried to create safety and access to enough resources to survive by working together in hunter-gatherer groups. This has taught us that it is often wise to help out others because this will increase chances of them helping you when you need it. These mechanisms are particularly influential in interdependent social networks, even today. Therefore, another way to make use of these mechanisms, in promoting sustainable decisions and behaviour, is to ensure that you create such a network as the context for these decisions and behaviours. By purposely creating a community feeling linked to the products, services and experiences they offer to customers, companies could tap into principles such as reciprocal altruism and social obligation, but also group reputation and group identity, in seducing potential customers to buy and consume sustainable alternatives.

This also links to the second tendency: our desire for relative status. If making sustainable decisions and displaying sustainable behaviour can be turned into something with which you can show you are successful, smart, willing to self-sacrifice and so on, they can be turned into something that people can use to increase their relative status. Ranking companies based on their sustainability efforts could encourage them to do more. Consciously *not* decreasing the price of sustainable products, possibly even increasing them, could actually better persuade some consumers to buy them than doing the opposite. It surely seems to work for Tesla, who have managed to turn their electric cars into status symbols rather than transportation that only attracts 'tree huggers'.

Similarly, our tendency to copy the behaviour of others, our predisposition to be short-sighted and our proneness to disregard impalpable concerns can all be used to promote sustainability. Based on these principles, it makes no sense to communicate how many people are *not* behaving sustainably, and how this is ruining our climate in the long run. Therefore, it would help to change the message into one that shows how many people *do* make sustainable decisions and display sustainable behaviour, especially if those include well-known and popular role models. It would also help to make environmental and social problems predictable, visible and tangible. Griskevicius *et al.* (2012) actually use the examples of colouring harmful emissions and altering the taste of water to represent the level of pollution to illustrate how this could be done. Maybe these examples are not always realistic, but they do highlight the relevance of our senses in comparison to complex statistics and detailed but abstract predictions.

Shaping hospitality contexts that favour sustainability

Which brings us to the hospitality industry's role in all this. Surely, if any industry should be able to find ways to create 'messages and incentives that reach [our] [. . .] ancestral sensory mechanisms' (Griskevicius *et al.*, 2012, p. 124), it would be the hospitality industry. If any industry is able to turn sustainable behaviour into something fun and exciting, it must be this one. If context is so important for our decisions and behaviour, this is the industry you would turn to for creating contexts that can make specific decisions and behaviours feel logical, pleasant, worth it, and so on. If these companies can make you feel like you have stepped into a completely different world, like theme parks do, or make you forget about your daily worries and completely unwind, like holidays and resorts do, why could they not use the same talents, qualities and circumstances to create the perfect conditions to discuss sustainability and experience the benefits of more sustainable decisions and behaviour?

Simultaneously, the previous chapters have indicated that hospitality businesses and professionals have so far been rather reluctant to focus on creating those conditions, contexts and links between their core product and sustainability. One of the explanations is that, for some reason, over time, the relationship that lies at the heart of the hospitality industry, the relationship between host and guest, seems to have evolved into a barrier rather than a catalyst for furthering sustainability in this industry. A recent study (Melissen *et al.*, 2016) suggests that quite a few hospitality professionals are convinced that their customers are solely driven by hedonic and gain motives. In other words, they feel their customers do not want to be bothered with sustainability, and just want to enjoy their stay, visit, dinner, night out, and so on. Interestingly, a follow-up study performed by the same authors shows that this perspective on the hospitality industry's customers might very well be overly pessimistic (Cavagnaro *et al.*, 2018). In fact, it shows many customers are actually quite willing to sacrifice some comfort, that they would like to be involved in sustainability decisions of the company offering hospitality experiences to them, and that they would be inclined to actively participate in making sustainability measures and initiatives a success. They would certainly like to know more about what the company is doing or not doing with respect to sustainability, and why. However, they do have some doubts about whether hospitality businesses and professionals really want to pursue sustainability.

This is in line with a number of studies reported on in scientific journals and popular media over recent years. Overall, we, the general public, are more and more aware of the seriousness and urgency of the sustainable development challenge our societies are faced with. We also feel that something needs to change. However, we are both reluctant to step up to the plate and be the first to act, and we have serious doubts about the motivations of others to make the *right* choices for the *right* reasons. Somehow, we assume our own values, norms and beliefs with respect to the need to achieve sustainable development to be different from those of others. This lack of trust in other people's normative goals, especially when it comes to sustainability, is part of the explanation of why we usually persist in making selfish choices in situations that represent social dilemmas.

However, if we all feel that way, this would imply that we are all open to changing our decisions and behaviour. We are not *against* sustainable development; we just find it difficult to step up to the plate. All of our brains have Stone Age elements that can hinder us in making sustainable decisions and engaging in sustainable behaviour, but can also be used to take down those barriers. We all struggle with conflicting goals but we are also susceptible to environments and contexts that help us resolve these conflicts. Hospitality contexts are not the exception to this rule. Hospitality professionals and customers are not the only ones distrusting each other's motives and motivation. Therefore, there is absolutely no reason why the lessons learnt from the previous sections could not be applied in a hospitality setting. It just takes someone to take the first step, communicate openly and honestly about that, look for the right balance in combining the various approaches to stimulating sustainable decisions and behaviour, and, most importantly, not hesitate to ask for support.

The authors of this book firmly believe that hospitality professionals should feel perfectly comfortable with doing so. The whole idea of this industry is to create interactions between host and guest that benefit both. In a society that slowly but surely is changing into one in which sustainability is a must rather than just one of the options, being the one that takes the lead in furthering sustainability of this industry can only increase your long-term social licence to operate (Warhurst, 2005). Your core product is perfectly suited to resolve potential conflicts between hedonic, gain and normative goals. Your customers want you to at least give it a good try. And finally, this is what you have been trained to do: designing, staging and managing hospitality experiences that instil positive, fond memories in your customers' minds (Smit and Melissen, 2018). Surely you can do the same for experiences that are more sustainable, both with respect to their immediate impact and their influence on your customers' decisions and behaviour, both at your facility and once they return to their homes.

CASE 3.2

BUFFET

Introduction

Building on the success of the SDGs, Pacific Asia Travel Association (PATA) launched an awareness campaign – BUFFET – on food waste for the hospitality industry in 2017. The aim of the campaign is to drive positive change. The dedicated website offers a toolkit with information and resources on how to reduce food waste within your organisation. What is particularly good for businesses, is that it offers practical solutions per topic on food waste, e.g., 'I have too much food waste' and then one can click on the tip for 'Streamline deliveries' to get more information.

How can BUFFET lead to more pro-environmental behaviour?

BUFFET focuses on a combination of two approaches discussed in this chapter. When looking at creating a context for guests that stimulates them to not waste food, a few things can be done:

- Portion control
  - o Do not offer bread and/or other starter options prior to the meal or at the beginning of the buffet. In that way, guests are inclined to finish whatever they eat afterwards.
  - o Serve smaller portions and carefully weigh those portions. Please note that research has shown that reducing meat portions leads to less waste on meat plus an increased intake on vegetables.
  - o Offer different portion sizes to different guests, to fit different needs.
  - o Be more flexible with side dishes, e.g., size or price.

- Service and presentation
  - o Serve food on smaller plates to make the portions look larger.
  - o Present food in an attractive way, e.g., colourful.
  - o Present food creatively, reducing the quantity served.
  - o Use inedible parts of fruit and vegetables for garnishes.
  - o Use voluminous garnishes, e.g., curly salad leaves – same volume, fewer leaves.

- Communication with guests

  o It is vital to communicate changes to your practices as well as food waste reduction to your guests.
  o Raising awareness about food waste automatically decreases the amount of food waste.
  o Ask the guest questions, when taking the order, on portion size, ingredients or allergies, preferred cooking methods and side dishes, and read back the order. All of this reduces frequency of plates being sent back.

So what?

It is evident that these practical tips and solutions offered by BUFFET can create a context in which guests can be or are stimulated to make different, more sustainable, choices. This could not only lead to less food waste but also creates an opportunity for a stimulating a more sustainable, perhaps healthier, lifestyle for the guest, also after leaving your premises.

Source: PATA, https://www.pata.org/food-waste/

SUMMARY

Based on reading this chapter, we hope you will understand and remember the following:

- Why it is important to focus on human behaviour when you want to achieve sustainable development.
- The attitude-behaviour gap of humans in relation to sustainability.
- The concept of the tragedy of the commons.
- The concept of a social dilemma.
- The five behavioural tendencies that hinder sustainable behaviour but can also be used to promote sustainable alternatives:

  o self-interest;
  o desire for relative status;
  o copy others' behaviour;
  o short-sighted;
  o disregard intangible concerns.

- Transparency is key if you want to influence sustainable behaviour.
- Mind the different types of values.
- Convincing customers to accept or prefer sustainable alternatives needs to be based on combining three approaches:
  - utilitarian approach;
  - social/psychological approach;
  - system of provision approach.
- Hospitality businesses are perfectly positioned to create the right context for more sustainable decisions and behaviour.
- Customers are willing to sacrifice comfort and would like to be involved in sustainability decisions, measures and initiatives.

FOOD FOR THOUGHT

Based on the content of this chapter, the following questions, challenges and topics could serve as interesting starting points for further discussion:

- Think of a situation in which sustainable alternatives were offered and how the context influenced your decisions and behaviour.
- List three personal values and categorise them according to the types of goals discussed in this chapter.
- How would you create the right context in a hospitality business to promote sustainable behaviour?

References

Ajzen, I. (1985). 'From intentions to actions: A theory of planned behavior'. In J. Kuhl & J. Beckmann (eds.) *Action control* (pp. 11–39). Heidelberg: Springer.

Ajzen, I. & Madden, J.T. (1986). 'Prediction of goal-oriented behavior: attitudes, intentions, and perceived control'. *Journal of Experimental Social Psychology*, 22, 453–474.

Cavagnaro, E., Düweke, A. & Melissen, F. (2018). 'The host–guest relationship is the key to sustainable hospitality: lessons learned from a Dutch case study'. *Hospitality & Society*, 8(1), 23–44.

Dawes, R.M. (1980). 'Social dilemmas'. *Annual Review of Psychology*, 31(1), 169–193.

Dawkins, R. (1976). *The selfish gene*. New York: Oxford University Press.

Fishbein, M. & Ajzen, I. (1975). *Belief, attitude, intention, and behavior: an introduction to theory and research*. Reading, MA: Addison-Wesley.

Griskevicius, V., Cantú, S. & van Vugt, M. (2012). 'The evolutionary bases for sustainable behaviour: implications for marketing, policy, and social entrepreneurship'. *Journal of Public Policy & Marketing*, 31(1), 115–128.

Hall, M.C. (2013). 'Framing behavioural approaches to understanding and governing sustainable tourism consumption: beyond neoliberalism, "nudging" and green growth?' *Journal of Sustainable Tourism*, 21(7), 1091–1109.

Hardin, G.R. (1968). 'The tragedy of the commons'. *Science*, 162, 1243–1248.

Maloney, M. P. & Ward, M. P. (1973). 'Ecology: let's hear from the people: an objective scale for the measurement of ecological attitudes and knowledge. *American psychologist*, 28(7), 583.

Melissen, F., Cavagnaro, E., Damen, M. & Düweke, A. (2016). 'Is the hotel industry prepared to face the challenge of sustainable development?' *Journal of Vacation Marketing*, 22(3), 227–238.

Smit, B. & Melissen, F. (2018). *Sustainable customer experience design: co-creating experiences in events, tourism and hospitality*. New York: Routledge.

Smith, A. (1776, 1976). *The wealth of nations*. Chicago, IL: Chicago University Press.

Steg, L., Bolderdijk, J.W., Keizer, K. & Perlaviciute, G. (2014). 'An integrated framework for encouraging pro-environmental behaviour: the role of values, situational factors and goals'. *Journal of Environmental Psychology*, 38, 104–115.

Thaler, R.H. & Sunstein, C.R. (2008). *Nudge: improving decisions about health, wealth and happiness*. London: Yale University Press.

Warhurst, A. (2005). 'Future roles of business in society: the expanding boundaries of corporate social responsibility and a compelling case for partnership'. *Futures*, 37(2–3), 151–168.

Wilson, E. (2006). *The creation: an appeal to save life on earth*. New York: W.W. Norton and Company.

CHAPTER
4 Identity and sustainability

Introduction

The previous chapter has shown that it is not impossible to steer con-sumers' decisions and behaviour in a sustainable direction. In fact, it has demonstrated, and explained why, hospitality professionals should feel perfectly comfortable with doing so. The general public is increasingly aware of the seriousness and urgency of the sustainable development challenge – and research shows that those who consume hospitality experi-ences are no exception to this trend. Hospitality contexts also constitute especially interesting contexts for promoting sustainable decisions and behaviour, even after consumers have left these facilities and have returned to their daily lives, homes and jobs. What is more, focusing on consumers' needs and wishes, interacting with them based on accounting for their values and preferences, and shaping optimal contexts for doing so, is exactly what hospitality professionals have been trained to do. For most of them, it is what they like to do and why they have chosen to pursue a career in the hospitality industry. Simultaneously, as a company, your customers' values and preferences are not the only ones to take into account in the way you pursue sustainability, and how you involve your customers in doing so. It is also crucial to account for the core values of your company. This chapter explains why and, more importantly, highlights some key reference points and guidelines for aligning your company's identity with your customers' identity within the context of making a contribution to achieving sustain-able development of our societies. Finally, it explains and explores the key role of your staff in doing so.

Hospitality experiences, identity and values

The previous chapter has explained how exploiting Earth's resources has both benefitted us and is threatening our very existence. Even in a book on promoting sustainability in hospitality, maybe even especially in such as book, it is important to not only focus on the latter but to also acknowl-edge the former.

Consumption and identity

It is crucial to understand how technological developments, and the associated changes in our socio-economic system, which is now basically governed by principles such as capitalism and democracy, have changed our lives in many ways. Whereas in the *old* days many of our decisions and behaviours were the logical consequences of our upbringing, our family views, our community's characteristics and social norms, our social status, and so on, these days many of us *enjoy* a lot more freedom with respect to the education and career we want to pursue, which religion we adhere to – if any, our political views, how we spend our leisure time – which has increased considerably, our money – most of us also have a lot more to spend, and so on (Smit and Melissen, 2018). Simply put, who we are and what we (want to) do has more and more become a personal choice instead of something that is predetermined. This change is often referred to as a (still on-going) process of individualisation and implies that, in this day and age, an individual's identity is not fixed or predetermined but rather reflects something that they construct and communicate themselves, for instance through the products, services and experiences they consume. Just consider what somebody's chosen car tells you about them. A Volvo station car communicates something very different to us about an individual's identity, what they find important, what they value, than a Porsche 911. Someone who chooses to go to a vegan restaurant usually has different priorities than someone who *treats* him or herself to dinner once a week at that restaurant famous for its spare ribs. A guest staying in a five-star hotel in a city centre, during his or her holiday, is telling us something different about his or her preferences than someone who spends his or her holiday at a camp site in the middle of a natural park.

Even though what you are and what you do has increasingly become a personal choice, this does not change the fact that humans are social creatures. As is illustrated by Maslow's hierarchy of needs (1943), we not only have basic needs, such as oxygen for breathing, food and shelter, but also psychological, social and esteem needs. These relate to aspects such as the need to be loved, to feel like you belong, to be part of a group, as well as the need for respect and appreciation from others regarding who you are and what you do, especially the respect and appreciation of members of the group you (want to) belong to. As indicated earlier, important ways to communicate to others which group you (want to) belong to, but also which groups you definitely do *not* (want to) belong to, are the products, services and experiences you buy and consume. This could involve buying and consuming a particular brand of products, visiting particular concerts, staying in particular hotels, wearing particular (branded) clothing, and so on (Smit and Melissen, 2018). Using your consumption pattern to prove who or what you are or want to be, also in relation to others, is called symbolic consumption (Denzin, 1992; Giddens, 1999). Hospitality experiences can play a crucial role in this type of consumption. First, because we have more leisure time and more (financial) resources than ever before, many of us actually spend a significant amount of time and resources on buying and consuming the experiences staged by the hospitality industry. Second, these experiences are much better suited to express who we are and what we find important than most other products and services we buy and consume. Telling your friends you visited a casino and won €400 sends a much more powerful message than telling them what brand of toothpaste you use to brush your teeth. A story about you buying a candy bar at a gas station on the way to work is not going to have quite the same effect on your colleagues as a story about you bungee jumping at the theme park you visited over the weekend.

Values

Although we might all have similar basic, psychological, social and esteem needs, we all behave differently, even in similar circumstances. The concept of values appears to be crucial in explaining this. Values can be defined as enduring and relatively stable beliefs about which modes of conduct and end-states of existence we prefer (Rokeach, 1973). In other words, values relate to what we find important in life and how we want to behave to realise those things. As such, values 'serve as guiding principles in people's lives' (Schwartz, 1992, p. 21). Typical examples of values that link to what we find important in life are freedom, equality and family safety, whereas honesty and cheerfulness, but also intelligence and ambition, represent examples of values that link to our behaviour. A helpful tool in portraying people's so-called value system or set of values is the 'List of Values' (Kahle et al., 1986), which can be used to differentiate between (groups of) people through clustering them based on how they rank the following values: self-respect, sense of accomplishment, being well-respected, security, warm relationships with others, sense of belonging, excitement/fun and enjoyment in life, and self-fulfilment. Obviously, knowing and understanding the value systems of your (potential) customers is crucial for deciding on the segment(s) of potential customers you will be targeting and fine-tuning the specifics of the ultimate experience you will be staging for them. As Smit and Melissen (2018, p.51) put it: 'there is really no point in trying to design and stage the ultimate bungee jump experience for people with high scores for security and low scores for excitement'.

This very same logic applies to promoting sustainable decisions and behaviour of your customers. For instance, the previous chapter highlighted the relevance of accounting for the fact that, in many situations, three different and oftentimes-conflicting goals — hedonic, gain and normative goals — seem to play a role in what we decide and do. Promoting sustainability needs to account for these goals by either resolving the conflicts between them or purposely strengthening (the impact of) one of them. In doing so, it is important to realise that the goals that drive people in a particular situation, as well as the strength of the various goals, are not only dependent on the situation but also on people's values. In fact, Steg et al. (2014) point out that a person's values 'affect the way a person perceives a situation: which information is salient, how important different aspects of choice options are to people, and how they evaluate different aspects of the situation so that some actions and potential outcomes are seen as attractive whereas other actions are seen as aversive' (p. 108). They also indicate that decisions and behaviours that are relevant from a sustainable development perspective are usually influenced by a person's so-called self-enhancement values, which link to valuing one's own individual interests, and self-transcendent values, which link to valuing collective interests. Within the first category, you could distinguish between hedonic values, which link to a key concern for minimising effort and optimising your feelings, and egoistic values, which focus more on protecting or increasing your resources. For the second category, you could distinguish between altruistic values, focusing on the welfare of others, and biospheric values, which link to caring for nature and the environment.

Obviously, hedonic and egoistic values are closely linked to hedonic and gain goals respectively, whereas altruistic and biospheric values link to normative goals. In their paper on the influence of these various values on our decisions and behaviour, Steg *et al.* (2014) conclude that situational cues and stimuli can not only strengthen and weaken our focus on specific goals directly but also indirectly, through activating or deactivating our various values. It is beyond the scope of the discussion here to review the various mechanisms at work here in full detail. However, it is important to note that this, for instance, implies, as already highlighted in the previous chapter, that promoting sustainable decisions and behaviour is often not just a matter of making particular decisions and behaviour more fun, easier and cheaper. As a company, you would probably not convince people with strong self-transcendent values to buy or consume your sustainable products, services or experiences if you promote them solely based on these characteristics. That is simply not what they are looking for. They probably do not mind more fun, easier and cheaper – who does? – but these products, services and experiences do not help them to build and communicate their identity as a person who cares for others and the environment. Therefore, this is not the symbolic consumption they are looking for!

Your (sustainability) identity as a company

Given that consumers increasingly use their consumption pattern as a means to prove who or what they are or want to be, also in relation to others, businesses and professionals need to account for what their products, services and experiences, as well as the contexts they create for buying and consuming them, tell those same consumers about what they value, what they consider to be important. As a company, more and more, you have to consider the fact that consumers will not buy and consume those products, services and experiences from just anyone.

Understand your brand prism

A useful tool to account for the symbolic element of the consumption patterns of your (potential) customers is the so-called brand prism (Kapferer, 1997). This tool uses the analogy of a lens to analyse how (potential) consumers will likely interpret your decisions, actions, products and *contexts*. In other words, how they feel about you as a *brand*. A brand is not just represented by the ultimate product, service or experience, also not just by a name or logo indicating who has produced, delivered or staged it, but also by the source behind all of that (Kapferer, 1997). As such, a brand determines the identity associated with specific products, services or experiences. Consequently, a brand is often considered to be more like a living organism rather than just the name identifying the maker of something, and the identity of a brand is much like the identity of a person; it deals with values and preferences. As an individual business or professional offering products, services or experiences to consumers you always represent a specific brand, regardless of whether you operate as part of a bigger whole, for instance as a local establishment of a multinational company with a formal brand name and logo, or as an independent business, such as an independent restaurant or hotel. The principles included in the brand prism apply to both situations.

The first part of applying the brand prism framework is to use a so-called *internalisation* lens to assess how your brand represents a particular personality and culture, as well as a particular perspective on what your brand can do for (potential) customers' self-image. Obviously, your brand's personality relates to your identity as a business or professional. It could probably best be described as the set of (human) characteristics that could be assigned to you based on the way you communicate about yourself and your offer. The language and symbols you use are key to this personality. Your brand culture links to your values, as a company, and incorporates aspects such as what you would and would not do, or what you find important or acceptable. Together, your personality and culture need to be attractive to consumers within the context of symbolic consumption. Consumers will only buy and consume your products, services or experiences if your personality and culture add value to who and what they want to be; their self-image. If consumers want to be seen as hip and trendy, they are much more likely to have lunch in a lunchroom that they consider to be hip and trendy as well, rather than a lunchroom, café or restaurant that they consider old-fashioned or traditional.

Whether or not consumers will consider you to be hip and trendy is based on how you present yourself to (potential) customers. What are the physical facets that make your brand recognisable? These could involve your logo and the appearance of your facilities but also the furniture in your facilities or the colours of you staff's uniforms. Another aspect of your presentation is your behaviour. How does your staff interact with customers? How do you respond to complaints? And finally, there is the so-called reflected customer: how do you portray your typical customer, for instance, in your commercials or on your packaging? Together, these three elements – physical facets, relationships and the reflected customer – represent the *externalisation* lens.

It is crucial to create a coherent brand, not only to attract the *right* customers but also to ensure that their *expectations* are in line with what you (want to) offer them. If your restaurant is located in a historic building in a fancy neighbourhood in London and your waiters wear traditional black uniforms, do not be surprised that your diners expect you to treat them with respect and to keep a certain professional distance. If your waiters suddenly start acting rather informal and insist on using diners' first names in talking to them, chances are you will not like those diners' reviews on TripAdvisor. Similarly, if the hospitality experiences you stage, as a business or professional, are all about excitement and surprise, it is probably wise to use images of excited and surprised people in your advertisements rather than images of people contently relaxing in the sun.

CASE 4.1

Joker ViaVia Network

Introduction

In 1971, after having travelled together, a few students came up with the idea to build an organisation of (part-time) tour guides with a focus on enriching themselves and others via meetings all over the world. This was the start of the Joker ViaVia Network, then called Karavaan (based in Belgium). Over the years, various suborganisations were founded with the aim to support sustainable tourism. All of them together operate under the name of Joker ViaVia Network.

So what does Joker ViaVia Network do to create their identity?

From the very beginning, the organisation has been based on altruistic values, such as wanting to meet others and doing *good* for others. This type of organisation is usually referred to as a social enterprise or societal business. By now, the Joker ViaVia Network has further increased its positive impact by supporting numerous local cultural projects in the destinations visited, and opening up travel cafés where travellers and the local community can meet. Also, the network cooperates with tourism educational centres (in local communities) to achieve sustainable tourism. Finally, they assist local communities in setting up additional social businesses by sharing their knowledge and expertise.

So what?

It is evident that the Joker ViaVia Network embeds their values into everything they do, which is also apparent from their website. Travellers are made aware of what sustainable travel entails and how the Joker ViaVia Network wants to make an impact, and how all this relates to the network's values. Their logo and the layout of the website is down-to-earth, which is perfectly aligned with who and what they want to be. However, if and when you are looking for interesting trips on their website, it does point out to you that 'you will return as a better version of yourself'. This may sound a bit highbrow or pretentious to some but it is exactly what this network is all about. Therefore, highbrow or not, the sustainability identity of this network is certainly coherent and transparent.

Source: Joker, www.joker.be

ViaVia Travellers Café, http://www.viavia.world/en/home

Create a coherent sustainability brand/identity

Obviously, the same logic can be applied to a company's brand/identity with respect to sustainability. It makes no sense to communicate to potential customers that you value the environment in your commercials and then disappoint those that were attracted to that message by not living up to those values in the context you create for staging experiences for them, as well as the actual experiences themselves. This context is not just shaped by the company's sustainability policies. It is also shaped by policies that are in place for all other aspects of day-to-day operations. In fact, the context is shaped by all decisions and behaviours of a company, regardless of whether these are directly linked to sustainability or not. In other words, the context for promoting sustainable decisions and behaviour by your customers is shaped by all of your decisions and behaviours, as a company, not just with respect to sustainability issues and not just right here, right now but also all of your (past) decisions and behaviours that have shaped your overall brand/identity as a company.

As Postma *et al.* (2013) explain, through referring to the work by Driessen (2005), some companies go for the safe option in most decisions they make, and have a high need for control, whereas others are all about risk taking and trying to create and chase new opportunities. Some companies base most of their decisions on logical frameworks and known concepts; others are used to reacting swiftly to developments in the outside world, and find it important and easy to rely on their intuition and cues from their social context. If you combine these two contrasts or axes into one overview, this creates a typology based on four quadrants, which Driessen (2005) has labelled the Pioneer, the Salesman, the Manager and the Professional. These labels relate to the typical characteristics of those in charge in such companies. Postma *et al.* (2013) have added colours and qualifications to these quadrants and together they give a clear overview of four possible and distinct organisational DNAs for companies.

Obviously, these four types of company also represent four very distinct overall brands/identities. For instance, a company in the left-bottom quadrant is all about caring for their customers, tradition and security. Based on the brand prism logic, as discussed earlier, this company's brand is built, over the years, based on a personality that is all about being reliable, relationships with customers based on caring for them and nurturing them, tradition and stability as the characteristics that are emphasised in the language and images they use in advertisements and on their website, and staff who care for customers based on a service-with-a-smile attitude. A typical example of such a company would be a traditional, luxurious five-star hotel in a historic building in a posh neighbourhood in a big city. This is not the type of company that would organise an afternoon of bungee jumping for its guests, would it?

The same logic applies to decisions and behaviour with respect to sustainability. It makes no sense for a company in 'the Pioneer' quadrant to not pursue advanced sustainability measures, and focus on known and tested measures instead. Setting new standards and challenging existing paradigms in all other areas and then only do what is strictly required from a legal perspective when it comes to sustainability, would not be a logical combination for this company. More importantly, (potential) customers will pick up on such inconsistencies! You simply cannot expect your customers to support you, and step up to the plate with respect to sustainability, if your overall identity and your sustainability identity are not aligned. If you, as a company, are a typical Salesman and you are able to turn problems into opportunities in all other areas, surely you can do the same with respect to sustainability? You will not get away with using the excuse that it is simply too complicated and too expensive.

All of this may sound rather abstract. Therefore, to illustrate the logic of what has been discussed in this chapter so far, consider the following (purposely extreme but unfortunately not at all unrealistic) example.

A luxurious resort is located in India. Management is rather disappointed in their guests' motivation to support and engage in sustainability measures and initiatives by the resort, for instance with respect to responsible water management – a key topic in this part of the world – and a local charity project they support that focuses on protecting tigers – a species vulnerable to extinction, also in India. Management cannot understand why guests are so reluctant to support them in their efforts with respect to these two topics; they just do not seem to care. Their reaction to water-saving showerheads has been complaining and showering longer, and almost nobody has donated to the charity project. Therefore, they have decided to no longer actively promote these projects on the website and reception staff will no longer ask guests whether they would like to donate to the tiger project. They do still feel it is their responsibility to do something and, therefore, will not get rid of the water-saving showerheads in all guestrooms in the resort and they will continue to use rainwater for flushing toilets. As business has been going well for some time now, they will also continue to support the tiger project financially; they will just do so without making a big fuss about it to guests.

You might wonder why guests are not jumping on the sustainability bandwagon in this resort. Well, the answer is pretty straightforward: the context created by the resort's management is all wrong for that. For instance, one of the activities available to guests in this resort is to ride an elephant! We will spare you all details on why this is wrong from a sustainable development perspective, an animal cruelty perspective, an ethical perspective, and so on. If you want to know more about things like limited space to move, not enough water and food, the effect of chains, just go online and search for 'elephant abuse'. However, most of you reading this book are probably already familiar with why riding elephants, but also swimming with dolphins or meeting tigers, is just plain wrong. In that case, you probably also understand why this particular resort, which also advertises these elephant rides on its website, is probably not the resort where you will find the highest percentage of people with strong self-transcendent values or, at least, that this particular environment is not going to activate the pro-environmental values of guests present.

Especially not, if you realise that this resort might be using water-saving showerheads and rainwater for flushing toilets but combines this with a huge waterpark on its grounds, with water play areas such as swimming pools, water slides, splash pads, an artificial surfing beach, and so on, as well as an all-inclusive concept with respect to eating and drinking. Elephant riding and a waterpark do not really send the message of being a Salesman company when it comes to sustainability, do they? *Eat-and-drink-whatever-you-want-because-it-is-paid-for* is not exactly the perfect environment to criticise people on how long they take to have a shower. Supporting a charity project to save the tiger comes across as confused at best, but probably as an alibi, to anyone who is at least still partially driven by normative goals amidst all of this. To top it off, management has now decided to start downplaying any sustainability initiatives the resort does take, and to no longer actively encourage guests to get involved. Not exactly the way to go if you are really serious about sustainability and seeking the support of your customers for pursuing it.

A coherent and transparent message

This example just shows, once again, how important it is to align your overall brand/identity and your sustainability brand/identity with the context you create for your customers. There is no doubt that technological advancements might assist you, as a hospitality business or professional, in reducing the negative environmental or social impact of the ultimate experience you will be staging for your customers and, if possible, you should make full use of those possibilities. However, the actual impact of those technologies, and all other sustainability measures and initiatives you could consider to take your company to the next level in this respect, are very much dependent upon the way you communicate about what you want to accomplish and why. Not only in words, for instance as part of official statements or on your website, but also in terms of what your decisions and actions, both current and past ones, tell others about your intentions, your priorities and your values. You cannot expect your customers to be driven by normative goals if you are not showing them you are as well. Activating their altruistic values is a mission impossible if it is perfectly clear that you do not really care about your own staff by underpaying them, making them work ridiculously long hours and badmouthing them.

All this also links back to something discussed in Chapters 1 and 3: honesty and transparency with respect to reporting on your sustainability impact and efforts. Clearly, greenwashing is not going to help gather support from your customers for taking sustainability to the next level. In fact, it is far more likely to do the opposite because customers can usually see right through it, and are probably going to become cynical rather than enthusiastic about any new plans or measures. However, downplaying your sustainability efforts, usually referred to as greenhushing or greywashing, is also not the way the go, as the example of the resort has shown. In fact, failing to clearly communicate about your actual sustainability impact and, especially, your intentions and efforts with respect to reducing your negative impact, or initiatives that could create a positive impact, can have a detrimental effect on trying to promote sustainable decisions and behaviour of your customers (in the long run). As Steg *et al.* (2014) explain, only focusing on hedonic and gain goals in your communication about your sustainable offer to customers, and the context you create for consumption, creates a very unstable environment for promoting sustainability. In such a situation, you are only activating values linked to those goals and you are only reinforcing the relevance of those specific goals in relation to your offer while deactivating values linked to normative goals and moderating their relevance. This actually makes it more difficult to involve those same customers in your (future) sustainability efforts and initiatives because they will have *learned* to associate your company and your offer with meeting hedonic and gain goals, not normative goals. It will also only make it more difficult to convince those customers that you, as a company, really care about achieving normative goals, such as making a significant contribution to achieving sustainable development.

With this in mind, let us return to the relevance of the various sustainability labels and certification schemes that companies could focus on, also within the context of the hospitality industry. As indicated in Chapter 1, some (corporate) clients would not book a room in your hotel or visit your premises if you cannot prove to live up to a certain minimum sustainability standard, for instance through qualifying for these labels or certifications schemes. These schemes can also prove helpful in other ways, for instance, as checklists for reviewing known sustainability measures and assessing the relevance for your specific situation, and thus serve as a source of inspiration. These are perfectly acceptable reasons to pursue a particular label or certification. However, their added value with respect to promoting sustainable decisions and behaviour of your guests, diners or visitors is limited at best. Most of them know that one of the reasons for having them is to ensure you qualify for business bookings. Many of them have also seen reports in the media on the fact that many of these labels do not really say that much about actual sustainability performance of a company.

Therefore, limiting your communication about your sustainability impact, intentions and efforts to displaying the logo of a particular scheme or label on your website, and focusing on the hedonic and gain components of your facilities and your offer to your customers in all other communication, is probably going to do more harm than good. It is certainly not going to activate your customers' self-transcendent values and reinforce their normative goals, and it is not enough to clearly communicate that you actually do care about sustainable development and not just about meeting a specific minimum standard because that has now become the norm in the industry. Another downside is that most labels and certification schemes focus almost exclusively on environmental aspects, and they ignore, or find it difficult to address, the social component of sustainability. Therefore, only using these schemes as inspiration for your sustainability efforts, and as the means to communicate those efforts, at best portrays you as a company that has a limited perspective on sustainable development and at worst alienates customers with strong altruistic values.

All of this underlines the importance of carefully reviewing your way of accounting for and communicating about your sustainability performance, efforts and intentions, especially for businesses and professionals in the hospitality industry. Given that the core product offered to customers, and the contexts shaped for actual consumption, typically incorporate explicit attention for aspects such as fun, pleasure, excitement, surprise, enjoyment and more – typical hedonic and gain goals – these companies almost automatically run the risk of overstating and over-activating values that hinder sustainability, and understating and deactivating values that promote it. Therefore, as a hospitality business or professional, it actually makes sense to put more emphasis on sustainability aspects in your communication, the experience you stage for your customers and the environment you create for staging it than downplaying sustainability as something that is just not compatible with what this industry is about and what customers have on their minds when they consider, buy and consume your offer.

This and the previous chapter have clearly shown that doing so it not at all impossible. It might take careful consideration and some effort but it is not a given that the hospitality industry needs to be the villain when it comes to sustainable development. As indicated in Chapter 2, it really is a matter of choice. The various principles and mechanisms discussed in this chapter and the previous one can very well be applied in a hospitality setting. In fact, as discussed earlier, the hospitality industry might actually prove the perfect setting to experiment with ways to make hedonic, gain and normative goals come together. It could be the perfect environment to let customers experience that sustainability does not have to be something negative, expensive, uncomfortable, difficult or unattractive. If hospitality businesses and professionals manage to do so, this industry could create a positive impact that moves well beyond merely reducing the water and energy use at hospitality facilities. It could turn this industry into a catalyst for achieving sustainable development of our societies, and transform the villain into a hero.

CASE 4.2

The Big Lemon

Introduction

In 2007, The Big Lemon was founded in Brighton. It is an eco-friendly bus operator, whose buses run on cooking oil. The Big Lemon recently also introduced two electricity-powered buses, charged by solar power. Their total fleet currently comprises 23 buses. Their business focuses on bus services run in Brighton, as well as bus hire, day trips and they also organise walks. From the very beginning, The Big Lemon has been funded by offering shares and bonds to members of the public. Therefore, it represents a so-called community interest company.

So what does The Big Lemon do to create their identity?

Even though the name The Big Lemon does not immediately steer your thoughts towards the topic of sustainability, it certainly does raise curiosity. When visiting their website, a bright yellow screen with a cheerful logo pops up. Their mission is clearly stated below their logo on top of the page, regardless of which part of their website you visit. The mission immediately makes clear what they stand for – 'Our mission is to enable everyone to get around their community in an affordable, enjoyable and environmentally-sustainable way'. It is a mission that is likely to attract the *right* customers. This is further strengthened by testimonials from members of the public who have already bought shares, indicating why they believe in The Big Lemon, such as:

- 'I want to see cleaner, quieter streets with air fit to breathe.'
- 'It is an ethical business which I would like to see succeed, and it pays a decent interest rate.'

They also clearly communicate a vision for 2030, which is focused on the community: 'By 2030 every community in the UK has access to affordable, sustainable transport, using zero-emissions vehicles powered by renewable energy and owned by the local community.' Thus, looking at their mission, their vision, their communication on social media, and so on, one could argue The Big Lemon is sending a coherent message.

Figure 4.1 Communication by The Big Lemon
Courtesy of: The Big Lemon

So what?

The Big Lemon could be argued to represent a clear example of the reference point that if you really do what you say you will do, you will get the (right) recognition. Community members keep investing in the company and The Big Lemon has already won 15 awards, all related to being a socially responsible business.

Source: The Big Lemon, www.thebiglemon.com

Do not forget your own people!

Speaking of heroes: this transformation cannot happen without involving your staff. If there is one industry in which employees, and not management, form a crucial element of companies' performance and long-term success, it is the hospitality industry. Its core product is all about interacting with customers, building relationships, understanding their values and priorities. Staging successful hospitality experiences is very much dependent on the skills, expertise and attitudes of the employees.

Sending the right message

Sustainable development is not just about saving our planet. As discussed in Chapter 1, it is also about the legitimate aspirations of people for an improved quality of life, and about meeting the needs of *all* people, not just the privileged ones. Unfortunately, Chapter 1 has also concluded that the hospitality industry has a rather questionable reputation when it comes to how many companies in this industry treat their employees. If the hospitality industry is going to transform into a hero with respect to achieving sustainable development, this situation needs to change. You simply cannot expect your customers to trust your sustainability story if the way you treat your own employees is sending a different message. Drawing upon the altruistic values of your customers, in an effort to involve them in a charity project aimed at supporting those in need in poor regions of our world, is not going to work if they notice that you are not valuing your own staff. If you want to create a believable brand or identity with respect to your contribution to achieving sustainable development, the signals you are sending through the way you treat your staff better match it. If you claim to care about resolving poverty, you better pay your staff fair wages. If you claim to support the aspirations of people across our globe for an improved quality of life, you must also accommodate for the needs and wishes of your own employees. Like anyone else, they also need to feel they belong and that they are respected and appreciated; they also need opportunities to develop themselves and realise their potential. If you honestly feel all people are equal and deserve the same opportunities, embrace diversity in your own human resources management. Simultaneously, saving our planet cannot be done without 'social inclusion, social justice and greater equity' (Washington, 2015, p. 107). The simple fact is that, if only through population growth, the environmental, social and economic dimensions of sustainable development are inextricable. What is more, altruistic and biospheric values might be separate values, but chances of finding someone with high scores for one and extremely low scores for the other are rather slim. Therefore, even if you (only) claim to want to make a contribution to saving our planet, it is not a good idea to ignore the interests of your own employees. The mechanisms described in this chapter, such as the logic of the brand prism, will at best result in a split image.

It is important to note here, for those that are still not convinced, that caring for your employees is not just the *right* thing to do from a sustainable development perspective, and the *smart* thing to do within the context of creating a coherent and transparent brand/identity that supports sustainability measures and initiatives. Caring for and investing in your employees is also likely to result in increased employee performance and productivity, more committed and motivated employees and, thus, in improved interactions between your staff and your customers, which in turn leads to satisfied customers (Kusluvan *et al.*, 2010). It is not just the *right* thing to do, it is also the *smart* thing to do, in every sense of the word.

Create the message together with staff

Simultaneously, just about any sustainability measure or initiative requires your employees to support it. They are the ones that need to make it work in day-to-day operations. Obviously, this further reinforces the need to value your employees, because chances are you will only be able to have them engage in, and make the most of, those measures and initiatives if they feel engaged with your company in the first place.

Sinek (2009) explains that, basically, the success of any company, project or initiative starts with *why*. Most companies are very clear on *what* they do but not as clear on why they do that. This also applies to sustainability. However, if you want your employees to really engage in your sustainability measures and initiatives, they need to understand why that is so important. You need to have a clear message, a good story that explains not only to customers but also to your own employees what your purpose is with respect to your sustainability measures and initiatives. A story that can inspire and motivate them to get on board; a message that makes sense to them, and that they will be happy and proud to share with customers. Clearly, the best way to ensure this happens is to actively involve them in developing this story and creating this message. Doing so, not only allows you to activate their self-transcendent values, thereby strengthening both the relevance of their own normative goals and the believability of the sustainability message they send to customers in their interaction with them. It also allows you to tap into their knowledge, experience and creativity for finding smart ways to tackle sustainability in the particular context of your company. In turn, it increases your employees' knowledge, experience and creativity in ensuring sustainability measures and initiatives come to life and making them a success.

Interestingly, your employees are living their lives in the very same societies that we have described as increasingly individualistic, earlier in this chapter. As any individual, your employees are also looking for ways to build their identity and to show who they are or want to be, as well as what group they belong to or want to belong to. This is where sustainability can actually assist you to engage your employees with your company. Seriously trying to make a significant contribution to achieving sustainable development, as a company, allows your employees to make a difference through doing their job. This is exactly what more and more employees want. A job that can provide 'alignment with one's own concept of self, values, virtues and morals' (Glavas, 2012, p. 19) is what today's employee is looking for. That is the beauty of it all. Whereas making the most of sustainability measures and initiatives requires engaged employees, focusing on sustainability is one of 'the most powerful pathway[s] for engaging employees' (Glavas, 2012, p. 20). Therefore, once again, involving your employees in defining and shaping ambitious sustainability measures and initiatives is not just the *right* thing to do; it is also the *smart* thing to do, in every sense of the word.

This is true for any company but maybe even more so for companies in the hospitality industry. One of the authors of this book talked to a restaurant owner recently and he made the following telling statement:

> Pay all the hours and overtime your employees work. The times of working 80 hours and only getting paid 38 hours is gone. Of course, this might bring extra costs, but what happens if and when your employees are dissatisfied and frustrated because you do not reward [and appreciate] them for their work? They will quit their job and in the long run this will cost even more. Let's transform the hospitality industry *back into* one that is attractive to work in.

If anything, this chapter has shown that focusing on sustainability could assist companies in doing so. Sustainability need not be a threat; it is the *right* and the *smart* thing to do.

SUMMARY

Based on reading this chapter, we hope you will understand and remember the following:

* Nowadays, who we are and what we (want to) do is a personal choice instead of something that is predetermined.
* The concept of symbolic consumption and the role the hospitality industry can play.
* Why and how value systems could help you define target groups and experiences.
* How the principles of the brand prism framework help to shape a coherent sustainable brand/identity.

- How the four types of organizational DNA help to choose sustainability measures and initiatives that are in line with your brand/identity.
- It is necessary to communicate to your guests about sustainability and this communication needs to move beyond displaying the logo of a certification scheme.
- Transforming into a sustainable business cannot happen without involving your staff.
- Employees need to be treated well and in line with your values.
- The message of why and how you engage in sustainability measures and initiatives needs to be created together with staff.
- Employees are increasingly looking for a job with meaning/purpose; sustainability can assist in creating meaningful jobs.

FOOD FOR THOUGHT

Based on the content of this chapter, the following questions, challenges and topics could serve as interesting starting points for further discussion:

- In which company or job were you treated the best, and why?
- Which brands do you affiliate yourself with the most, and why?
- Name three brands that have a clear sustainability brand/identity.
- What are you looking for in a (future) job?

References

Denzin, N. (1992). The many faces of emotionality: reading persona. In C. Ellis & M. Flaherty (eds.) *Investigating subjectivity: research on lived experience* (vol. 139) (pp. 17–30). London: Sage.

Driessen, M.P. (2005). *E-Scan ondernemerstest: beoordeling en ontwikkeling ondernemers competentie.* [The entrepreneur scan measuring characteristics and traits of entrepreneurs. Netherlands: Entrepreneur Consultancy] (dissertation). Groningen: University of Groningen.

Giddens, A. (1999). *Runaway world: how globalization is reshaping our lives.* London: Profile Books.

Glavas, A. (2012). 'Employee engagement and sustainability: a model for implementing meaningfulness at and in work'. *Journal of Corporate Citizenship*, 46, 13–29.

Kahle, L.R., Beatty, S.E. & Homer, P. (1986). 'Alternative measurement approaches to consumer values: the list of values (LOV) and values and life style (VALS)'. *Journal of Consumer Research*, 13(3),405–409.

Kapferer, J-N. (1997). *Strategic brand management: creating and sustaining brand equity long term*. London: Kogan Page.

Kusluvan, S., Kusluvan, Z., Ilhan, I. & Buyruk, L. (2010). 'The human dimension. a review of human resources management issues in the tourism and hospitality industry'. *Cornell Hospitality Quarterly*, 51(2),171–214.

Maslow, A.H. (1943). 'A theory of human motivation'. *Psychological Review*, 50(4), 370.

Postma, A., Spruyt, E. & Cavagnaro, E. (2013). *Sustainable tourism 2040: a manifesto*. Leeuwarden: European Tourism Futures Institute.

Rokeach, M. (1973). *The nature of human values*. New York: The Free Press.

Schwartz, S.H. (1992). 'Universals in the context and structures of values: theoretical advances and empirical tests in 20 countries'. In M. Zanna (ed.) *Advances in experimental psychology* (vol. 25) (pp. 1–65). Orlando: Academic Press.

Sinek, S. (2009). *Start with why: how great leaders inspire everyone to take action*. New York: Penguin Group.

Smit, B. & Melissen, F. (2018). *Sustainable customer experience design: co-creating experiences in events, tourism and hospitality*. New York: Routledge.

Steg, L., Bolderdijk, J.W., Keizer, K. & Perlaviciute, G. (2014). 'An integrated framework for encouraging pro-environmental behaviour: the role of values, situational factors and goals'. *Journal of Environmental Psychology*, 38, 104–115.

Washington, H. (2015). *Demystifying sustainability: towards real solutions*. London: Routledge.

5 Your role in the community

Introduction

The previous chapters have highlighted the crucial role of people in pursuing sustainability, especially within the context of the hospitality industry. If hospitality businesses and professionals are to fulfil their potential to serve as catalysts for achieving sustainable development of our societies, they need to involve their customers and staff in doing so. However, the values and preferences of your customers and staff are not the only ones you need to consider and account for in the way you, as a hospitality company, (will) pursue sustainability. For a number of reasons, which are explored in detail in this chapter, it is also extremely important to establish a sustainable – in every sense of the word – relationship with your immediate environment, such as the neighbourhood in which you are located, the region in which you operate, and the natural environment surrounding your facilities. In fact, the train of thought presented in the subsequent sections suggests that sustainability measures and initiatives by hospitality businesses and professionals quite simply *have* to be rooted or embedded within the particular context created by their immediate surroundings for them to be truly successful from a sustainable development perspective. This is not to say that specific measures and initiatives cannot focus on making a contribution to resolving global or local problems in different parts of our world. However, the overall message you are sending with respect to *why* you are pursuing sustainability and *how* you want to do so, as a company, through your assortment of actual measures and initiatives, the way you have integrated them in your strategy, tactics and day-to-day operations, as well as the way you communicate about them, cannot ignore the *local* within the so-called 'global-local nexus' (Saarinen, 2006, p. 1134) of sustainability. This would undermine its believability, support for what you (are trying to) do, and, ultimately, your social licence to operate and your actual contribution to achieving sustainable development. The remainder of this chapter explains why, and highlights a range of opportunities to actually tap into local developments and so-called grass-roots movements as a key foundation for your sustainability efforts.

Reasons for a local orientation

This section explores why a focus on the *local* is so important for the hospitality industry to boost its contribution to achieving sustainable development. Before doing so, a warning to you, our reader, is in order though. Some of these reasons move well beyond the daily practicalities of hospitality operations, and some of them link to issues such as the lock-in effect of our current socio-economic system and the urgent need to create and experiment with viable alternatives. Therefore, bear with us while we review this wide variety of arguments. We promise to put them in a coherent and practical perspective in the next section.

Concerted action is not happening

Any company trying to contribute to achieving sustainable development needs to account for its surroundings in doing so. It simply makes no sense to contribute to resolving problems in other parts of the world at the expense of causing more (sustainability) problems in your own neighbourhood, region or ecosystem. As discussed in Chapter 1, sustainable development comprises an ethical and a systemic dimension. In some way or another, all of our local, regional and global social, environmental and economic systems are connected and intertwined. Adjusting the unsustainable course of our societies requires accounting for these interdependencies. Simultaneously, we, humanity, have so far found it rather difficult to implement comprehensive measures that improve sustainability of all of these systems at once. We will return to this issue in more detail later in this chapter and the next one. However, it is important to note here that the tourism industry, of which the hospitality industry is an integral part, represents a particularly telling example that illustrates these difficulties. Efforts to improve the sustainability of the tourism industry have not yet resulted in any drastic changes with respect to global 'institutions, norms, rules, structures and infrastructures' (Hall, 2013, p. 1099) that together shape the so-called system of provision. As discussed in Chapter 3, this complicates changing the lifestyles, social practices and consumption patterns of those involved.

To illustrate this, just consider flying. Airplanes still emit significant amounts of greenhouse gases and a technological solution for this problem is not on the horizon. Air travel is also relatively cheap and available to ever-growing numbers of tourists. Consequently, greenhouse gas emissions associated with tourism air travel are rapidly increasing. Meanwhile, despite symbolic milestones such as the Paris Agreement on climate change, politicians and the business world have not yet shown any apparent interest in changing this situation – for instance through taxes or increasing prices to reflect actual damage done by flying. Weaver (2011) describes this situation as a 'failure of the international community to arrive at a consensus for concerted action' (p. 13). Like many others, the authors of this book included, he expects that this will not change soon, and certainly not in time to avoid some of the detrimental effects of the current system of provision. That is why he suggests, as do more and more researchers and other advocates of sustainability initiatives, that companies in the tourism industry are better off focusing on local initiatives, and 'participatory exposure of residents and tourists' (p. 13) to those initiatives, as the way forward to make any significant contribution to achieving sustainable development.

Obviously, as an integral part of the tourism industry, this also applies to the hospitality industry. What is more, hospitality companies are perfectly positioned to create such participatory exposure. A tour operator or airline company might find it rather difficult to set the right sustainable example, and to create opportunities for tourists and residents to jointly experience sustainability in a positive way. This is very different for a restaurant or a hotel. They often have both tourists and residents as their customers. They are also trained in designing, staging and managing experiences that prompt positive feelings, based on interactions between people. Therefore, as discussed in the previous chapters, if any company could create the right circumstances to bring tourists and residents together and convince them to buy and consume more sustainable experiences, but also stimulate both groups to make more sustainable decisions and engage in more sustainable behaviour, even *after* consuming these particular experiences, it would be a hospitality company.

Hospitality as a natural stakeholder

However, even without referring to the failures of the international community to tackle unsustainability of the tourism industry at a global level, one could argue that a local orientation with respect to sustainability efforts is almost self-evident for most hospitality companies. A significant portion of their (potential) negative impacts from a sustainable development perspective is local. As discussed in Chapter 1, just consider the impact on local ecosystems and wildlife of a resort located in a pristine natural environment. There are many other examples, such as traffic jams caused by visitors to an event or theme park, nuisance caused by guests of an accommodation located in the middle of a residential area, and the detrimental effect of opening a new hotel on the income of bed and breakfasts operated by local residents.

However, hospitality companies are very much intertwined with local communities in many more ways than just through their (potential) negative impacts. As noted in the previous chapter, oftentimes hospitality companies also host residents as their customers; local residents might dine in a restaurant or have their morning coffee in a hotel lobby. Hospitality companies usually employ local residents as their staff. They might also buy (some of) their supplies from local businesses and the other way around. In any case, hospitality companies are the neighbours of local residents and cannot help but influence their daily lives in that way. This influence need not be all negative. In fact, a train of thought that has always been part of discussions on sustainable hospitality and the wider concept of sustainable tourism is the potential of these companies to bring prosperity to local communities and their residents. Notably, the United Nations proclaimed 2017 as the International Year of Sustainable Tourism for Development based on the reasoning that tourism could play an important role in generating economic growth, and in reducing poverty in parts of our world. If organised properly, this positive impact could move beyond merely providing a direct income to local residents and businesses but could also serve as a catalyst and/or co-financer for improving local infrastructure, social services and social cohesion (projects). As noted by Smit and Melissen (2018), sometimes tourism can help raise awareness and financial means to preserve and protect local ecosystems and wildlife, for instance, if the money spent by tourists is used to fight poaching. By creating jobs and income for local residents, these companies also make an indirect contribution to the same cause through creating circumstances in which these residents do not have to rely on poaching as their livelihood.

All this illustrates that the statement made in Chapter 1, claiming that hospitality businesses and professionals represent *natural* stakeholders and partners in sustainable development of local and regional social, environmental and economic systems, is by no means an exaggeration. Maybe more so than any other type of company, hospitality companies are inevitably linked to them, both through their (current) negative impacts and their (potential) positive impacts on all stakeholders involved, including the natural environment. Therefore, they *naturally* play an integral role in any attempt to make these systems more sustainable. Consequently, it would be almost *unnatural* for hospitality businesses and professionals to not (also) apply a local orientation to their sustainability efforts.

The local is your and your customers' context

All that was discussed in the previous chapter further reinforces the need for a local orientation in your decisions and behaviour, as a hospitality company, with respect to sustainability. Creating a coherent sustainability brand/identity is crucial in making your sustainability efforts a success. An important part of this brand/identity is communicated to your customers, regardless of whether they are tourists from another part of the world or local residents, through the context in which you stage your experiences for them. This context is shaped by all of your decisions and behaviours, not just those directly related to your sustainability efforts. Just consider the example of the luxurious resort in India, discussed in the previous chapter. In the end, it really does not matter whether the exact spot where your guests can pay for and start their elephant ride is within or just outside the border of your premises. It is still part of the overall context in which they consume their experience of enjoying a holiday in a resort in India. Therefore, decisions and behaviours, as well as situational cues and stimuli, that are formally not part of the experience your hospitality company offers to customers, still very much influence the overall context for your customers, as well as your staff, and can thus seriously strengthen or weaken specific goals and activate or deactivate specific values that are extremely relevant from a sustainability perspective.

CASE 5.1

Four Seasons Bali

Rob van Ginneken and Jasper Bosma

> For and on behalf of Four Seasons Resort Bali at Jimbaran Bay and Sayan Ubud, we deeply apologize to all Hindus for offense and disappointment that was caused by the Karma Cleansing program that was held in our property, which contained Hindu rituals. The organisation of the program was not intended to cause disrespect, or harassment to Hindus, but it was no more than our misunderstanding of the impact of that program causing discomfort for Hindus. For that, we have stopped the program, and furthermore we will always coordinate with all related parties. We will always commit to keep the Ajeg Bali (preserve Bali) by respecting the religion, custom, culture, and tradition of locals. Thus our open apologies we convey. Thank you.
>
> (Wockner and Erviani, 2015)

The above statement was issued by the General Manager of the Four Seasons Resort Sayan, on the island of Bali, Indonesia, in September 2015. According to articles on Australian news website News.Com (Wockner and Ervani, 2015a and 2015b), the Hindu Karma Cleansing ceremony performed on two homosexual men created quite the local backlash. Several organisations, such as the Grand Council of Customary Villages and the Bali Wedding Association, called for investigation of the matter. The governor of Bali even went so far as to call the event a disgrace for Bali.

The Four Seasons Resort Sayan is an exclusive resort located in the Ayung River Valley. The resort, managed by the well-known luxury hotel operator Four Seasons, caters mainly to western affluent tourists, staging hospitality experiences against the backdrop of traditional Balinese nature and culture. Organising weddings on the resort grounds is part of their extensive range of hospitality services. What caused the events described here was a picture, posted on Facebook, of what appeared to be a wedding ceremony between an Indonesian man and a Westerner, and performed by what seemed to be a Hindu holy man, at the resort. It went on to attract the attention of the local authorities, tourism-related stakeholders and the general public. Wockner and Ervani (2015b) even report the couple received threats and described the public reaction to the event as *a national outcry*.

According to Indonesian law, marriage should always happen between a woman and a man. Same-sex marriage is punishable, according to Indonesian authorities, because of strong religious norms against it. The majority of the Indonesian population is Muslim; however, on the island of Bali, where the resort is located, the majority is Hindu. While Islam unambiguously rejects homosexuality, Hinduism is not that clear on the subject, and opinions strongly vary among Hindus. While traditionally Hinduism does not support homosexuality, relationships between same-sex individuals are recognised, and in Hindu art, both males and females are found depicted in same-sex intercourse. Practising homosexuality is, since 2009, legal in India, where the majority of the population is Hindu. All of this may partly explain why Bali has been a popular destination for gay couples.

Following the picture gaining widespread attention and causing such a strong local response, Four Seasons explained that the ceremony held at the resort was *not* in fact a wedding, but rather a Hindu Karma Cleansing Ceremony, called Melukat. However, the Bali authorities were unimpressed and charged the sales executive of the hotel with blasphemy, which is punishable by a jail sentence of up to five years. According to the police, wedding organisers, such as those at the Four Seasons, should be aware of the importance of the Hindu symbols, and while they could have accepted a Bali-themed ceremony, the use of religious symbols for celebrating same-sex marriage would still be considered blasphemy. Still, according to the police, the sales executive should have known that (traditional) Hinduism defines marriage as between a man and a woman, and should therefore have refused to organise the ceremony.

The police later discovered that the couple in question had already requested to marry in the resort a year earlier. At that time, the hotel refused to organise the wedding and the couple married legally in the US before returning to the hotel to request the Karma Cleansing ceremony, which triggered the above-mentioned local stir. Soon after the ceremony, the couple left the country to travel back to the US.

Sources:
Wockner, C. & Erviani, K. (2015a). 'Bali police name Four Seasons Resort sales executive as a suspect in gay wedding investigation'. *News. Com.* Available on http://www.news.com.au/world/bali-police-name-four-seasons-resort-sales-executive-as-a-suspect-in-gay-wedding-investiga tion/news-story/ffb168fa6d85dccca9c173e8df827418. Last accessed 11 October 2017.
    Wockner, C. & Erviani, K. (2015b). 'Controversy after gay marriage wedding in Bali'. *News.Com.* http://www.news.com.au/world/asia/ controversy-after-gay-marriage-wedding-in-bali/news-story/1e6744df3a f250aaa067531bd99a740e. Last accessed 11 October 2017.

Simultaneously, most hospitality companies employ local residents as their staff. In the previous chapter, it has been concluded that involving your staff in defining and shaping your sustainability measures and initiatives is the right and the smart thing to do. Given that your employees live their lives in the local community, it is only logical that they will (also) focus on local sustainability problems as the problems they would like to resolve through the sustainability efforts of your company. If they experience poor air quality in their neighbourhood, this is the environmental problem they are likely to want to tackle first. If your company were located in a poor neighbourhood or region, in which many of your employees' relatives and friends struggle to earn their livelihood, it would be silly to expect them to come up with the idea of saving an endangered species of monkeys living thousands and thousands of miles away.

Interestingly, a local orientation also seems to play an increasingly important role in choices made by tourists, and in the experiences they favour. More and more of us seem to have left the idea behind us that holidays are about escaping reality, and increasingly we are looking for authenticity and local cultures, customs and products as key ingredients of the contexts in which we want to spend our valuable leisure time. Information technology and social media have also made it much easier to explore and connect to the local communities we visit, and to share our thoughts while doing so with those that are looking for similar experiences. Today's typical tourist is not looking to avoid contact with the real world; he wants to immerse himself in everyday environments (Russo and Dominguez, 2016). This is one of the explanations for the ever-increasing popularity of concepts such as city trips, couchsurfing and Airbnb. It is also an important reason why more and more restaurants focus on local specialities and local produce. In the book *Reinventing the Local in Tourism*, editors Antonio Paolo Russo and Greg Richards (2016), and all authors who contributed chapters, explore some of the mechanisms at work here. It is beyond the scope of this chapter to review all of these mechanisms in detail. However, it is important to note here that one of the lessons that can be learned from Russo and Richards' exploration is that today's consumers, in their roles as tourists and consumers of hospitality experiences, are not only looking for more authenticity but also for meaningful, personal experiences; we want to be more than spectators and want to be active and creative (Forno and Garibaldi, 2016). In other words, we are no longer *leaning back* and waiting for hospitality providers to stage their experiences for us and serve us (with a smile); we want to co-create those experiences, and an important part of that is to actively explore and connect to the communities in which those hospitality providers are located.

In other words, a local orientation is key for almost all decisions you make as a hospitality business or professional, also, and maybe even especially, with respect to your sustainability efforts. It is an integral part of the context in which you stage your sustainable hospitality experience, and thus of your sustainability brand/identity, but also of the context in which you try to engage your staff in doing so and of the overall experience an ever-increasing portion of your (potential) customers is looking for.

The only way is (bottom-)up!

However, the particular characteristics of the tourism and hospitality industries are not the only reasons why sustainability efforts need to apply a local orientation. As stated in Chapter 1, achieving sustainable development will have to involve quite drastic changes to the way we distribute wealth across our globe, what we consider to be our needs and appropriate ways of meeting them, our technological systems, our production systems, and more. Unfortunately, we are finding it very difficult to make these changes.

Chapter 3 has already highlighted how this is linked to mechanisms incorporated in the economic system that dominates most of our societies when it comes to the ground rules that businesses have to adhere to, how professionals in those businesses are *supposed to* make decisions, how those businesses interact with consumers and the decisions we expect from our politicians and policy-makers. These mechanisms are based on the principles of free market capitalism. Development of this system could be argued to be the direct result of technological innovations, such as the steam engine, combined with population growth, which allowed and required us to find more efficient ways to exploit our planet's resources to satisfy our needs. Over time, this has not only changed the way we exploit these resources, and thus our production system, but also our social system. Over the last two centuries, more and more of us moved to cities, more and more of us earn our livelihood by working as an employee in companies or other types of organisations aimed at producing the products, services and experiences we crave, and more and more of our relationships and interactions with other people are in some way or another founded in the exchange of money for goods (Smit and Melissen, 2018). At first glance, for many of us, this system – our current socio-economic system – seems to work pretty well because it has given us material wealth, freedom, health, opportunities to pursue our dreams, possibilities to shape and communicate our identity through symbolic consumption, and more. Not surprisingly, many of the values on which this system is based – such as promoting private property, autonomy and economic growth – and the ways to pursue them – through exploiting Earth's resources and aiming for increased efficiency, productivity and profits – have become logical, attractive principles in the minds of most of us (Laszlo, 2001; Melissen, 2016; Melissen and Moratis, 2016). In fact, most of us find it hard to imagine a socio-economic system that is not based on these values, if only because we have never experienced an alternative system and the current system is full of mechanisms, clues and stimuli that reinforce its goals and activate its values.

This explains why we are finding it so hard to make the changes necessary to achieve sustainable development. Simply put, our current socio-economic system comprises a number of self-reinforcing mechanisms that make it extremely difficult to change its functioning. For instance, our politicians need to make decisions that please us, the voters, to stand a chance of re-election. The only way they can do that is by ensuring that they have the means to make us happy: money. They need this money to create and maintain infrastructure and to provide education, health care, social welfare, safety, and so on. This money needs to come from taxes on products, salaries and profits. Consequently, they need to promote the exploitation of natural resources on which many of those products, salaries and profits are dependent. They need to promote economic growth to be able to continue to afford to pay for the welfare state to which we have become so accustomed and on which we have become so reliant. The proven recipe for doing so is to promote efficiency, productivity and profits. To add to all this, for quite a few countries in our world, a significant portion of government income is directly coming from taxing fossil fuels and selling oil, gas, coal and other natural resources to other countries.

Loorbach (2014) describes this situation as a lock-in; a situation in which 'we seem to be caught in a vicious cycle of optimising an inherently unsustainable system which closes down the space for the development of inherently better alternatives' (p. 31). In his book *The Craftsman*, sociologist Sennett refers to it as Pandora's Casket and states, in referring to the Greek myth of Pandora, that 'culture founded on man-made things risks continual self-harm' (2008, p. 2). Regardless of whether we call the situation a vicious cycle, a lock-in or Pandora's Casket, these references and reflections all boil down to highlighting the complications involved in changing the functioning of a socio-economic system such as ours. The way it is financed, how it is inextricably intertwined with power relationships and how it consistently reinforces gain goals and self-enhancement values of those *in power*, make it a system that does not support but rather blocks achieving sustainable development.

Obviously, this leaves us, humanity, in quite a pickle. The way we have always tackled problems is not going to help us achieve sustainable development. The way we have arranged our world to satisfy our needs is not going to help us meet our needs in the long run. In fact, it is the very reason why we are in trouble. This means we need a new approach; a new way of arranging our world to satisfy our needs. If our current socio-economic system not only hinders sustainable development but is also the cause for the unsustainable course of our societies, we are left with no other option than to create a new socio-economic system.

You might ask why we, the authors, felt the need to include this train of thought in a section on explaining the need for a local orientation in the sustainability efforts of hospitality businesses and professionals. The reason is that this same train of thought highlights that development of an alternative to our current socio-economic system is not likely to be instigated by those *in power* in our current system. Initiatives to create viable alternatives to our current socio-economic system are much more likely to come from so-called grassroots movements and civil society; from us, the people, and social movements and initiatives (Marques and Mintzberg, 2015). In fact, Loorbach (2014) claims that we can already witness the signs of a 'gradual and creeping revolution in which citizens, consumers, social entrepreneurs, civil servants, researchers and activists are changing the way in which we live, consume, produce in small but certain steps' (p. 35). This revolution is taking place in self-organised networks that draw upon their own resources, knowledge and capacities instead of relying on government or other parties *in power* in the *old* system to show us the way. These networks are based on values such as inclusiveness, equality and sustainable ways of using our natural resources to satisfy our needs. Typical well-known examples of such networks are the various platforms for sharing your house, your car, your tools and your food with others, such as Airbnb, Uber, Peerby and the food/meal sharing platforms mentioned in Chapter 2. However, there are many more examples of experimenting with new ways of living, consuming and producing already *out there*. Just consider the growing number of farmers who deliver sustainable energy generated by their wind turbines and solar panels (directly) to local residents, or groups of residents in urban areas that collectively invest in technologies for sustainable energy. In other words, creating and experimenting with sustainable alternatives to our socio-economic system is mostly accomplished through *bottom-up* innovation (Loorbach, 2014), not top-down. Many of the initiatives take place in (local) communities and (social) networks, are instigated by residents of neighbourhoods, and rely on the resources, imagination and knowledge of the members of those communities and networks (Melissen, 2016).

CASE 5.2

The New Parkway Theater

Introduction

The Parkway Speakeasy Theater in Oakland, California (US) used to be a popular place in the Oakland community. People got together to watch a movie, drink a beer and catch up with friends. In 2009, the Parkway Speakeasy Theater had to close due to problems that are typical for our current socio-economic system; a landlord and owners fighting over money. Local residents were very sorry to see the theatre go. In fact, they were so sorry that they decided to organise the *comeback* of the theatre themselves, through crowd funding. The theatre reopened late 2012 as the New Parkway Theater. The theatre has two screening rooms and a café.

So how does The New Parkway Theater link to the local community?

All activities in the New Parkway Theatre are very much community-focused. One example is the Karma Cinema program, which means that one night a week regular customers pay *whatever they want* for their movie ticket. At the end of each month, 20% of the revenues of Karma Cinema tickets are donated to local charities that serve local residents. The theatre also organises community-based activities, such as bingo, quiz and open-mic nights. When it comes to their staff, besides paying them a living wage, they also make sure that they share in profits and they make an effort to employ people who might find difficulty getting work in other places, such as ex-convicts. The New Parkway Theater is also concerned with their activities having an impact on the environment and therefore asks customers not to order more than they can consume and helps them in creating as little waste as possible, for instance through reusing metal straws. In terms of suppliers, they use local suppliers as much as possible, for example all their beers and wines come from within 200 miles. Furthermore, they also take health into account by not serving food that contains high-fructose corn syrup or palm oil.

So what?

The authors of this book would argue that the New Parkway Theater could be seen as a prime example of how a hospitality business could operate with a strong local orientation. This particular theatre is doing this in relation to both social and environmental aspects. What is more, it shows us how to create a new type of business model; one that is not just about making profit for the sake of making profit.

Source: The New Parkway Theater, www.thenewparkway.com

So, this actually brings us back to Weaver's (2011) words, mentioned earlier in this section. He suggests that companies in the tourism industry are better off focusing on local initiatives, and sustainability efforts that involve both tourists and residents (of local communities), in making a contribution to achieving sustainable development. As it turns out, this is not just true for tourism and hospitality. Local communities and social networks are the most logical and promising starting point for most sustainability measures and initiatives, not just those directly linked to hospitality operations. This is where people create and experiment with viable alternatives to our current socio-economic system. This is where you, as a hospitality business or professional, can 'tap into and join the already on-going but gradual and still mostly hidden [sustainability] revolution' and join forces 'with this movement of engaged citizens, entrepreneurs, civil servants, researchers and activists, some of whom might actually already be working for your organisation' (Melissen, 2016), who might be supplying you with the produce, products and services you need, or who simply live *next to you*.

Communities and networks

Together with these networks of engaged citizens, entrepreneurs, civil servants and other motivated parties, you can produce the type of collaborations that are crucial to creating and experimenting with sustainable alternatives to our current socio-economic system. As indicated earlier, doing so requires accounting for the interdependencies between social, environmental and economic systems, and also between the local, regional and global level. These experiments move beyond merely applying specific physical technologies, they require a holistic approach that combines such technologies with new social technologies (Laukkanen and Patala, 2014). They might involve some risk-taking, daring to not play by the rules of the *old* game and co-creating new norms and rules while playing the *new* game. They might very well involve discussing, and co-creating new ways of meeting, what we consider to represent our needs that must be satisfied by a socio-economic system. Together, all of these elements represent a challenge that an individual company should not take on in isolation. If you, as a company, want to contribute to rising to this challenge, you better ensure you have the support and help of relevant stakeholders. Simply put, the innovations required for creating and experimenting with sustainable alternatives to our socio-economic system are not only too complex to take on alone, they also reach well beyond the boundaries of an individual company (Bocken *et al.*, 2014; Rohrbeck *et al.*, 2013).

This, once again, reinforces the relevance, especially for hospitality businesses and professionals, of focusing on the type of initiatives put forward by Weaver (2011). If you, as a hospitality company, want to engage in co-creating the way *we* have arranged our world to satisfy *our* needs, it is important to realise that your ultimate product is already very much a so-called co-production or co-creation by relevant stakeholders. As highlighted earlier in this section, today's consumers, in their roles as tourists and consumers of hospitality experiences, want to be more than spectators and want to co-create those experiences, with an important part of that co-creation taking place through actively exploring and connecting to the communities in which a hospitality establishment is located. As Pappalepore and Smith (2016) explain, before, during and after consuming the actual hospitality experience(s) you stage for them, your consumers interact not only with you as a *company* (for instance, through visiting your website) but also with other consumers, friends, family, your staff and your neighbours – both local residents and local companies – both face-to-face and online. Their interpretation of how you have helped all of them satisfy their needs cannot be seen separately from all of these interactions. Ultimately, their experience, as a tourist or consumer of hospitality experiences, is the product of a co-creation process in which all of these stakeholders play a role. How this will affect their future decisions and behaviour is also the product of this same co-creation. This is also the case for the sustainability level of this ultimate experience and whether they will be willing and motivated to actively contribute to making it as sustainable as possible, the impact it will have on their future sustainability decisions and behaviour, and so on. Making this ultimate experience more sustainable, turning it into something that would fit in a sustainable socio-economic system, is therefore automatically also something that is based on a co-creation process that involves all of these stakeholders.

These same physical and virtual communities and networks are also the perfect place to have a *sensible* and *constructive* discussion on what *we* consider to represent *our* needs, and on sustainable ways of meeting them. For instance, this is the most promising environment to make use of some of the evolutionary tendencies, discussed in Chapter 3, to promote sustainability. The effect of copying the behaviour of others is proven to be the strongest in small communities and social networks. This is where (new) social (sustainability) norms could be developed without immediately being brought down (to *reality*) by concepts such as economic growth and possible trade deficits (between countries). This is also where you can more easily tap into principles such as reciprocal altruism, social obligation, group reputation and group identity for promoting sustainable decisions and behaviour. If the right people give the right sustainable example, there is every chance that this example will become the norm. If you help others to become more sustainable, there is every chance they will return the favour. Local communities are also the place where sustainability impacts can be (made) palpable, recognisable, visible, *real*. In other words, within the context of physical and virtual communities, it is much easier to build trust and communicate directly and openly, and thus to create the circumstances in which the evolutionary tendencies identified by Griskevicius *et al.* (2012) need not hinder sustainability but can actually be used to promote and pursue it. Interestingly, hospitality businesses and professionals are specialists in building trust, open communication and accounting for the needs and wishes of others, but also in the impact of the (physical) environment on how people feel and behave. Therefore, physical and virtual communities and networks are not only the logical starting point for their own ambitions with respect to contributing to achieving sustainable development. These businesses and professionals could also play a crucial role in setting up and preserving (the right atmosphere and circumstances in) these communities and networks, so that others also feel comfortable using them as the starting point for pursuing their own sustainability ambitions. If you combine this with the fact, as discussed earlier, that most hospitality companies are very much intertwined with local communities, all this puts them in the perfect position to be the ones that take the lead, or at least make a significant contribution, in (purposely) creating the networks needed for producing and experimenting with sustainable alternatives to our current socio-economic system.

Local orientation: a practical perspective

Admittedly, some of the concepts discussed in the previous section are rather abstract. Our socio-economic system is not something most of us are likely to reflect upon on a daily basis. We are not knowingly following the guidance of the invisible hand of the free market in most decisions we make. You probably cannot remember the last time you consciously made use of the reciprocal altruism principle, and you might find it rather difficult to come up with an example of a hospitality company that uses social obligation to promote sustainable behaviour by its customers. Therefore, as promised, this section puts all of this in a coherent and more practical perspective.

The reasons revisited

Maybe the best way to do so is to first take another look at the reasons for a local orientation, discussed in detail in the previous section, and try to summarise them succinctly here.

Hospitality is part of tourism, and tourism has a questionable reputation when it comes to sustainability. Probably the most widely known and debated issue within this context relates to flying. More and more of us fly, for instance, to enjoy our holidays in exotic locations but also for business trips and family visits. More and more people across our globe can afford to fly. Even though all of us, including those in charge of tax systems and regulations, such as policy-makers and politicians but also aviation and tourism trade associations, know very well that flying is a significant contributor to climate change. However, the total number of people flying is still increasing, and there are no rules, regulations or incentives in place to stop this. Unfortunately, there are quite a few more examples of unsustainable practices in tourism that the international community has been unable, or maybe unwilling, to put a stop to (yet) through regulation. As an individual hospitality business or professional, chances of you being the one who will be able to turn things around at this (global) level of decision-making, and organise concerted action by all relevant stakeholders, is slim to none. Obviously, you could use this as an excuse to not engage in sustainability efforts at all. However, this really does not mean that there is nothing you can do. In fact, there is no reason why you could not engage in sustainability efforts at a local level. Maybe, as an individual hotel or theme park, you cannot stop people from travelling to your facilities by airplane, but you *can* encourage those same people to travel from the airport to your location by public transport, or by using sustainable transport organised by you. Maybe, as an individual restaurant or conference centre, you cannot force the whole industry to act as employers that truly value their employees, and as good neighbours for people living and working in the same neighbourhood, city or region, but you *can* be a good employer for your own employees, and you *can* be a good neighbour for people living and working in your own local community or region. In fact, the latter really is a no-brainer because many of those people are also your customers. If anyone can set the right example and create circumstances that would stimulate both your customers and your neighbours to follow your example when it comes to sustainability, it would be you. You know how to get through to people, how to listen and talk to them, how to make them feel happy and open to new ideas, solutions and behaviour. This is what you have been trained to do. This is what hospitality is all about.

Unfortunately, the way hospitality is organised today is known to also cause quite a few negative impacts on that same local community, also from a sustainability perspective. Therefore, the logical starting point for you, as a company that wants to make a contribution to achieving sustainable development, is to take away or, at least, minimise these impacts. However, you do not have to stop there. Given that you are so closely connected to the local community, you could also have a positive impact. You could assist members of your community with their sustainability efforts, or you could set up joint measures and initiatives. Doing so will only benefit your own efforts, measures and initiatives because it will create an environment full of signals and stimuli that reinforce the importance of sustainability, and thus an environment in which it also becomes much easier to involve your own customers in those efforts, measures and initiatives. Given that a number of your employees live their lives in your local community also makes it that much easier to involve them in pursuing sustainability – they will not only be doing the *right* thing during their working days, and become more motivated as a result of that, but they will also be the ones reaping the benefits when they return to their homes.

What is more, all of this will only improve the overall experience of your customers. This is what more and more of them are looking for; they do not want to be served, they want to explore and connect to what is happening in your neighbourhood. Therefore, they *want* your sustainability efforts to be focused on the local community and your direct (natural) surroundings. Doing so will only increase the chances of them wanting to support your efforts, and also the chances of them remembering and applying lessons learnt once they return home.

Interestingly, lessons learnt in other sectors and industries, and with respect to other types of sustainability problems and solutions, all seem to boil down to the very same principles. The logical starting point for truly making almost all of the changes needed for achieving sustainable development is local communities and social networks. This is where we can learn to live, produce and consume in ways that do not harm others and our environment. This is where most of us feel safe enough, trust others enough, and feel comfortable to communicate openly and honestly enough to discuss alternatives to *bigger, faster, more exclusive* and *more quantity*. This is also where you will find people who have already experimented with doing things differently, and who have already acquired quite some expertise with respect to what works and what does not.

Once again, as a hospitality business or professional, you should feel perfectly comfortable in joining forces with this grassroots movement. It is all about building trust, relationships, networks, reciprocity and accounting for each other's needs and wishes. You know how to do that. As an expert on hospitality experiences, you know how to get through to people, how to listen and talk to them, how to make them feel comfortable and open to new ideas, solutions and behaviours. Joining or even (assisting in) setting up these networks should feel *natural* to you. You could be of great help in making these communities and networks a success, and thus in making a contribution to changing the way we, as humanity, have organised our world to satisfy our needs into an arrangement that is based on inclusiveness, equality and a responsible way of interacting with our natural environment. In earlier chapters, the potential of the hospitality industry to serve as a catalyst for achieving sustainable development of our societies has been highlighted repeatedly. The train of thought presented in the previous section suggests that applying a local orientation to your sustainability efforts, as a hospitality business or professional, is likely to be *a*, or maybe even *the*, requirement for realising this potential.

CASE 5.3

SeQuential Biofuel Station

Introduction

SeQuential (SQ) Biofuels is a company founded in 2002 by two men who met whilst having pizza at a restaurant. Those two men both had a passion for the outdoors, the environment and the belief that there is a more sustainable way of creating energy. Ultimately, this passion resulted into producing local, responsible bio-products, such as biodiesel by refining used cooking oil. Two places where you can fuel your car with biodiesel and fuel yourself with food are their refuel stations in Eugene, Oregon (US). The stations are also referred to as SQ Hubs, with a neighbourhood market and a community café offering fresh, natural and local food.

Figure 5.1 SQ Biofuel Station, also known as SQ Hub
Courtesy of: SeQuential Biofuels

So how does SeQuential Biofuel Station link to the local community?

First of all, SQ only works with local companies to provide the fuel. In everything they do, they want to support small businesses in their state. They also built the stations from regionally sourced materials and use renewable energy from solar panels. They also have a living roof to reduce heat and cooling costs. The products sold in their market and café are all local, e.g., local beer and wine, locally roasted coffee beans. SQ encourages environmental behaviour from local people by selling products from Klean Kanteen, which is a company focusing on re-usable bottles and flasks. Furthermore, they work with partners, such as a local sustainable seafood company, offering their customers discount on sustainable seafood products.

So what?

SeQuential Biofuel Station is an example of the *blurring* of boundaries. A fuel station is no longer just a fuel station, but also a place where people get together and where good food is provided. This is especially novel for a fuel station, as they are often infused with standardised assortment. SQ is intrinsically motivated to make a change and is integrating this into their business model. As they state themselves: 'Expect friendly faces'. If that is not hospitality . . .

Source: SeQuential Biofuels, www.sqbiofuels.com

Practical examples

Obviously, the details of applying a local orientation to your sustainability efforts, as a hospitality company, really depend on the characteristics of the community in which you are located, the natural environment that surrounds you or the social network you belong to (or have created). If your local community is troubled by unemployment and poverty, it seems logical that this orientation will make you focus more on the social component of sustainable development. In contrast, consider a hospitality company that is surrounded by nature and wildlife, which is both slowly but surely starting to show the consequences of the unsustainable course our societies are on. Especially if the natural environment and wildlife are important reasons for customers to frequent this establishment, and thus also crucial to the long-term livelihood of staff and other local entrepreneurs, you would expect this company to pay (extra) attention to protecting this ecosystem and fighting the causes for its deterioration. Then again, the actual measures and initiatives that your company will focus on, in making a contribution to what is obviously a priority in your community or network, also need to account for your expertise, your track record, your value proposition – what particular hospitality experience you offer to your customers, your customers' preferences and priorities, your staff's preferences and priorities, and so on. As explained in the previous chapters, all of these elements need to come together in your sustainability identity, and your overall identity, as a company. Simply put, this whole *picture* needs to make sense to all stakeholders involved for you to be able to make an optimal contribution to achieving sustainable development. Therefore, it is virtually impossible to provide a detailed guideline or checklist here that would show every individual hospitality business or professional what they need to focus on in their sustainability efforts, and how to do that.

Instead, the final subsection of this chapter concludes with some practical examples of sustainability topics/issues that hospitality companies could address, based on applying a local orientation and possible avenues for doing so. Hopefully, these examples can serve as inspiration.

One of the most obvious areas in which joining forces with a local community or social network could open the door to improving your sustainability performance, beyond what you could achieve as an individual company, is *energy*. As discussed in Chapter 2, there is a wide range of (technological) solutions that could be applied to reduce the use of non-renewable energy. Some of these solutions might not be feasible for your company but could become available to you if you cooperate with other local companies or local residents, farmers and so on. For instance, suppose you would like to apply solar energy or wind energy to provide for your energy needs. It could very well be that the roofs of your facilities do not allow for installing solar panels because the construction is not suitable for it, or because it would mean the panels would not be facing the sun. Putting a huge wind turbine on your premises might also be problematic because buildings that block the wind surround your establishment, or local residents living close to you would not appreciate such a huge construction in their line of sight from their garden. However, it could very well be that some of these buildings, maybe even the houses of those local residents, are actually perfectly suited for installing solar panels. Why not collectively invest in solar panels, boilers, plumbing and more, so that all of you can use the hot water and energy created. You could do the same for geothermal resources to heat or cool your facilities and those of other local companies and the houses of local residents. If there were factories or farmers in the region in which you are located, maybe they would have space to install wind turbines that can generate electricity that can be used by the local community. Quite possibly, there are opportunities to also use so-called waste heat from those factories or the greenhouses of those farmers to set up a low temperature district heating system.

Obviously, in some instances it could also be the hospitality company that is the one with the perfect circumstances to apply specific solutions or technologies, and to *share* the resulting *heat* or *electricity* with the neighbourhood or region. For instance, as a theme park you might very well have buildings suitable and space available for solar panels and wind turbines. The Eden Project in Cornwall, UK, represents an example of such a theme park. This park hosts pop concerts, and includes gardens, exhibition centres and two huge domes with numerous plants. It has actually been set up as a theme park that educates visitors on the relationship between people and plants in a pleasant and fun environment and way. It is still a hospitality company though, that survives on making a profit through staging a hospitality experience for paying customers. However, it also purposely contributes to raising awareness about environmental problems and solutions. Within the context of the discussion here, one of the interesting initiatives that this theme park engages in is to join forces with external funders to build a geothermal power plant that could provide not only the theme park but also some 5,000 homes of local residents with energy.

Another interesting example is a project in the city of Utrecht in the Netherlands, where both residents and local entrepreneurs, including a number of hospitality companies such as bed and breakfasts, lunchrooms, cafés and restaurants, are involved in setting up a local energy system that not only applies solar panels and wind turbines but also uses batteries in the homes and establishments of participants, even in their (electric) cars (!), to store energy that is not needed immediately. Obviously, it is well beyond the scope of this book to review all physical and social technologies that are already or could be applied for decentralised production, storage and distribution of renewable energy. However, it would be fair to say that the examples mentioned here are just the tip of the proverbial iceberg of possible arrangements that could assist in moving away from a socio-economic system that is heavily reliant upon fossil fuels, and in developing one that is based on a responsible way of interacting with our environment with respect to providing it with the energy it requires.

Obviously, similar principles can be applied with respect to, for instance, *food*. Why would the produce used to prepare meals served in restaurants, hotels and other hospitality establishments have to be flown in from across our globe? Why is it so crucial to serve strawberries when it is wintertime in your region of the world? Fortunately, more and more customers are perfectly fine with eating what the local natural environment can produce without using pesticides and other unnatural assistance. In fact, more and more of us actually prefer local, seasonal and organic. More and more hospitality providers have realised, and are proving, that using such produce is not going to decrease the overall hospitality experience staged for their customers; quite the opposite. Obviously, the latter is also closely linked to what has been discussed earlier in this chapter. More and more consumers of hospitality experiences do not want to be served just anything; they want to explore and connect to what is happening in your neighbourhood and region. This also means that they increasingly expect hospitality companies' sustainability efforts, including those linked to food, to have a logical link to the local community and the direct (natural) surroundings. Once again, the options to shape such efforts are numerous. Hospitality companies could grow their own food, have vertical or rooftop gardens, join food waste and food sharing initiatives in their neighbourhoods or set them up themselves, and more.

As with energy, as a hospitality company, you could join forces with other local companies, local residents, grassroots movements and so on, to transform (local) food production and consumption systems. While doing so, maybe you could contribute not just to creating new energy and food production and consumption systems but also have other positive impacts on local people and nature. A nice example of the latter is the Four Seasons Resort Bali, who have joined the bee conservation and community enterprise program Plan Bee in Indonesia. This grassroots movement brings together local companies, residents, farmers and forest honey gatherers in fighting the decline in local bee populations. The Four Seasons Resort has created vegetable and herb gardens on their premises for local, seasonal and organic produce they use in meals served to their guests, but they also have two beehives with more than 10,000 bees in total. Guests not only can enjoy the bees' labour through the honey that is used in meals, cocktails and even spa treatments but they are also educated about the threat facing bees, the impact of the decline in bee populations on ecosystems and our food production systems, and how they can help protect bee populations. This project not only helps bees – and through bees whole ecosystems – but also local residents by teaching them how to earn their livelihood based on gathering and selling honey in a sustainable way, thus protecting their long-term livelihood. As with energy, this is just one example of the many, many ways in which a local orientation with respect to food could create opportunities for hospitality businesses and professionals to truly make a contribution to revolutionising our global food production and consumption systems through bottom-up innovation and collaboration in local communities.

Besides food, hospitality companies could *share* many other things with other members of local communities and social networks, such as tools, (electric) cars and space. The latter could be a crucial element of a hospitality company's contribution to achieving sustainable development. A beautiful example of this principle is the concept of the so-called diffuse hotels or *albergo diffuso* in Italy, in villages or small towns that are increasingly depopulated as a result of industrialisation and urbanisation (Gilli and Ferrari, 2016). These hotels are not located in one dedicated building but rather comprise several spaces within such a village or town; either single rooms or suites or multiple rooms and suites located in various existing buildings that have been abandoned by their original owners or occupants. Restoration of these (parts of) buildings to create accommodation for tourists, instead of constructing new hotels or resorts, means that significant amounts of natural resources are saved. What is more, these diffuse hotels can *bring back life* to those villages and towns through reactivating the local economy and creating a livelihood for local residents and entrepreneurs. This effect is not necessarily limited to providing jobs to local residents in the hotel itself but could also be through bringing in additional customers for other types of businesses in the local community.

Once again, tourists visiting these villages and towns are likely to be looking for authenticity, exploring traditional local culture and activities, and connecting to people living there. This opens the door, so to speak, to revitalising these regions based on reusing and reactivating existing spaces, buildings and crafts, local cuisine based on local produce, and so on. This revitalisation generates income that can be used to further ensure local infrastructure and ecosystems are preserved and protected. Ultimately, from a sustainable development perspective, this form of creating *new* destinations and accommodation for ever-increasing numbers of tourists is a far better option than constructing new accommodation, roads and attractions that not only require more natural resources in the form of materials, energy, water, and so on, but may also require disturbing or even sacrificing yet another of the last few unspoilt habitats of rare animal species or vulnerable ecosystems in the region.

Obviously, there are many more ways in which a local orientation for sustainability efforts by hospitality businesses and professionals could create interesting opportunities from a sustainable development perspective. By employing their expertise with respect to interactions between people, and regarding how to account for people's preferences, needs and wishes, hospitality companies could play a crucial role in promoting *social cohesion* in neighbourhoods in which local residents have become estranged from each other. They could create and offer jobs to people with a so-called *distance to the labour market*, which further assists in revitalisation of and social cohesion in, for instance, *impoverished neighbourhoods*. Maybe hospitality businesses and professionals could assist in tackling some of the negative impacts of urban *overtourism*. If anyone would have the expertise needed to create environments that make people feel welcome, it would be these businesses and professionals; why could they not contribute to, or even take the lead in, projects aimed at making local residents feel at home again in their own city instead of having the feeling they are living their lives in an over-crowded theme park because of urban tourism getting out of hand? Maybe the example of diffuse hotels can offer inspiration for tackling the problems associated with Airbnb in many cities in our world; could hospitality businesses, professionals and principles assist in persuading, assisting or *seducing* both the owners of these types of accommodation and the tourists staying there to make different choices, and to engage in different behaviour that would benefit not only them but also local residents and our natural environment?

All of the examples mentioned in this section show that a local orienta-tion could assist hospitality businesses and professionals in optimising their contribution to achieving sustainable development. In the areas of energy and food, but also with respect to water, material use, new technologies and many more topics, collaborating with local stakeholders and focusing on local priorities, impacts and circumstances can open the door to a world of opportunities, knowledge, expertise, support, resources and financial means that would not be available to an indivi-dual company acting alone. The description of the diffuse hotel concept represents a nice example of how principles and concepts such as the sharing economy, the circular economy, economic development, and preservation and protection of our natural world could not only be applied simultaneously but could also reinforce each other. More impor-tantly, it shows the potential of the hospitality industry in making this come true, and how doing so is probably best realised through applying a local orientation. Finally, the discussion on social cohesion, inclusive-ness, Airbnb and overtourism (in cities) highlights how sustainability efforts need not always focus on reducing a hospitality company's own (direct) negative impacts. These efforts could also comprise providing opportunities to those that need them, and focusing on committing your time, energy and expertise to projects or initiatives initiated or impor-tant to other local stakeholders.

Ultimately, as stated earlier, it is important that all of your efforts come together and contribute to creating a logical, coherent and appealing sustainability identity and overall brand for your company. You also need to be able to explain clearly to your customers, and to those with whom you would like to join forces, *why* you (are proposing to) do what you do, as well as *how* you (will) do so and *what* this will contribute to achieving sustainable development of (local) society. Trustworthiness, open and honest communication, perseverance, sometimes courage or even a willingness to take some risks, are crucial to all this. However, if you manage to account for all of these reference points, the list of opportunities to make a significant contribution to achieving sustainable development is almost endless. Many of these opportunities do not involve huge investments. Most of them simply require you to make the choice to make a (positive) difference. In the long run, the rewards are obvious: more satisfied customers, better relationships with local stake-holders, a healthier and more attractive natural environment, a sustained social licence to operate, more motivated and productive employees, to name just a few. To put it bluntly, using the excuse that sustainability is not rewarding, too expensive, not wanted, is just that: an excuse. It is not. It is a choice. It is the only logical choice, also, and maybe even especially, for hospitality businesses and professionals.

SUMMARY

Based on reading this chapter, we hope you will understand and remember the following:

- It is key to establish a sustainable relationship with your immediate environment.
- Hospitality businesses that want to make a change are better off focusing on local initiatives.
- Hospitality businesses are intertwined with local communities and represent a natural stakeholder for local measures and initiatives.
- Employees (often local residents) help you focus on local sustainability problems.
- Sustainability efforts depend on the characteristics of the community in which you are located.
- Tourists are increasingly looking for local orientation and meaningful, personal experiences.
- Tourists and guests want to co-create hospitality experiences and connect to local communities and social networks.
- Bottom-up innovation and grassroots movements are crucial to creating and experimenting with sustainable alternatives to our current socio-economic system.
- Hospitality companies could share many things with members of local communities and join forces with them in creating bottom-up innovation and grassroots movements.
- Sustainability efforts in or with your local community do not have to involve huge investments; they represent a choice; a logical choice.

FOOD FOR THOUGHT

Based on the content of this chapter, the following questions, challenges and topics could serve as interesting starting points for further discussion:

- Which sharing platforms do you know, and have you actively used them?
- What is a meaningful and personal experience for you when travelling, and does that experience involve the local community?
- In this day and age, what positive difference do you think hospitality businesses can make to their local environment?

Based on the Four Seasons Bali case 5.1:

- Indonesian law is, for a large part, based on religious beliefs. Some of these laws contradict the Universal Declaration of Human Rights. Does this mean the rights of local governments to enact and maintain such laws could be disputed?
- Should Four Seasons, the local sales executive, the holy man ... have known better? Isn't it the responsibility of such a renowned professional hotel operator to be (more) in touch with local sensitivities? How about the couple themselves: one of them being Indonesian, should he have known better?
- Why did the sales executive and Hindu holy man cooperate in the hotel staging this experience; an experience they probably *knew* would cause problems with the local community they were part of themselves?

References

Bocken, N., Short, S., Rana, P. & Evans, S. (2014). 'A literature and practice review to develop sustainable business model archetypes'. *Journal of Cleaner Production*, 65, 42–56.

Forno, F. & Garibaldi, R. (2016). 'Ethical travel: holidaying to fight the Italian mafia'. In A. Russo & G. Richards (eds.) *Reinventing the local in tourism: producing, consuming and negotiating place* (pp. 50–64). Buffalo: Channel View Publications.

Gilli, M. & Ferrari, S. (2016). 'The "diffuse" hotel: an Italian new model of sustainable hospitality". In A. Russo & G. Richards (eds.) *Reinventing the local in tourism: producing, consuming and negotiating place* (pp. 65–83). Buffalo: Channel View Publications.

Griskevicius, V., Cantú, S. & van Vugt, M. (2012). 'The evolutionary bases for sustainable behaviour: implications for marketing, policy, and social entrepreneurship'. *Journal of Public Policy & Marketing*, 31(1),115–128.

Hall, M.C. (2013). 'Framing behavioural approaches to understanding and governing sustainable tourism consumption: beyond neoliberalism, "nudging" and green growth?'. *Journal of Sustainable Tourism*, 21(7),1091–1109.

Laszlo, E. (2001). 'Human evolution in the third millennium'. *Futures*, 23 (4),349–372.

Laukkanen, M. & Patala, S. (2014). 'Analysing barriers to sustainable business model innovation: innovation systems approach'. *International Journal of Innovation Management*, 18, 1440010.

Loorbach, D. (2014). *To transition! Governance panarchy in the new transformation* (inaugural speech). Rotterdam: Erasmus University Rotterdam.

Marques, J. & Mintzberg, H. (2015). 'Why corporate social responsibility isn't a piece of cake'. *MIT Sloan Management Review*, 56, 7–11.

Melissen, F. (2016). *Fourth generation sustainable business models* (inaugural speech). Breda: NHTV Breda University of Applied Sciences.

Melissen, F. & Moratis, L. (2016). A call for fourth generation sustainable business models. *The Journal of Corporate Citizenship*, 63, 8–16.

Pappalepore, I. & Smith, A. (2016). 'The co-creation of urban tourism experiences'. In A. Russo & G. Richards (eds.) *Reinventing the local in tourism: producing, consuming and negotiating place* (pp. 87–100). Buffalo: Channel View Publications.

Rohrbeck, R., Konnertz, L. & Knab, S. (2013). 'Collaborative business modelling for systemic and sustainability innovations'. *International Journal of Technology Management*, 63, 4–23.

Russo, A. & Dominguez, A. (2016). 'The shifting spatial logic of tourism in networked hospitality'. In A. Russo & G. Richards (eds.) *Reinventing the local in tourism: producing, consuming and negotiating place* (pp. 15–34). Buffalo: Channel View Publications.

Russo, A. & Richards, G. (eds.) (2016). *Reinventing the local in tourism: producing, consuming and negotiating place*. Buffalo: Channel View Publications.

Saarinen, J. (2006). 'Traditions of sustainability in tourism studies'. *Annals of Tourism Research*, 33(4),1121–1140.

Sennett, R. (2008). *The craftsman*. New Haven, CT: Yale University Press.

Smit, B. & Melissen, F. (2018). *Sustainable customer experience design: co-creating experiences in events, tourism and hospitality*. New York: Routledge.

Weaver, D. (2011). 'Can sustainable tourism survive climate change?'. *Journal of Sustainable Tourism*, 19(1),5–15.

6 Your business model and competencies

Introduction

In the introduction to this book, the authors indicated that its chapters are all part of an overall storyline that could best be described as a call for action. The subsequent chapters have discussed our biggest and most urgent societal challenge – achieving sustainable development of our societies, the relevance of specific sustainability topics within the context of the hospitality industry, the role of technology versus people, how to account for people's decision-making and behaviour, the need for honest and transparent communication and involving staff in creating a coherent sustainability identity, and why it is crucial to focus on local communities, social networks and bottom-up innovation in efforts to improve sustainability in the hospitality industry. This final chapter is about connecting all the dots. It is now time to link all that has been discussed in previous chapters to the business models that need to be applied by companies in this industry, and to the competencies current and future hospitality professionals need to master to make it live up to its potential to serve as a catalyst for achieving sustainable development of our societies. And, obviously, it concludes with an invitation to those same professionals to take on this challenge. In fact, it would probably be fair to say that it is not so much an invitation but rather an urgent appeal.

Business models for sustainability

The train of thought presented in this book kicked off by highlighting that the hospitality industry could make a significant contribution to achieving sustainable development, not only by reducing or avoiding the negative impacts associated with its current ways of operating but also through creating positive impacts and serving as a catalyst for achieving sustainable development of wider society. With respect to reducing or avoiding its negative impacts, five key topics – energy, waste, water, food/drinks and building (design, materials and furnishing) – were reviewed, and two main conclusions followed from that review. First, pursuing sustainable development, also – and maybe even especially – as a hospitality company, need not be complicated and does not always require huge investments. In fact, oftentimes it simply requires deciding to do things differently; to make the choice to account for sustainability aspects in all decisions you make and all actions you take. Second, ultimately, sustainable development is probably not as much about technology as it is about people. Fully integrating sustainability principles into the core business strategy, tactics and operations of a hospitality company, and thus ensuring that all decisions and actions are indeed founded on sustainability principles, requires the support of a number of stakeholders.

First and foremost, you need the support of your customers. Obviously, if you cannot convince them to buy and consume your sustainable hospitality experiences instead of unsustainable alternatives, your contribution to reducing the negative impacts of the hospitality industry will be limited. Many of these hospitality experiences also require those same customers to make sustainable decisions and engage in sustainable behaviour to minimise their (direct) negative impacts or to create (direct and indirect) positive ones. The latter directly links to the potential of the hospitality industry to create a positive impact that moves far beyond the direct environmental, social and economic consequences of the experiences staged by hospitality businesses and professionals. If these experiences can stimulate customers to use more sustainable products and services, and engage in more sustainable behaviour, in their daily lives as well, their ultimate positive impact on achieving sustainable development of our societies could be very significant. All of this underlines the relevance of hospitality businesses and professionals purposely creating contexts that stimulate sustainable decision-making and behaviour, and communicating openly and honestly about why they are doing so and what they have accomplished (so far). Previous chapters have shown that this might be difficult, but that it is certainly not impossible.

However, this cannot be done without the support and involvement of staff. They not only play a crucial role in staging hospitality experiences, and thus in the sustainability message you send to your customers through staging them. Their knowledge, expertise, creativity, values and priorities are also crucial input for defining and shaping the *right* message for your particular company, and creating a coherent sustainability brand/identity that supports your sustainability ambitions and that aligns with your overall brand/identity. What is more, involving them in decision-making with respect to *what* you want to accomplish, *why* and *how*, is both the right and the smart thing to do, both from a sustainable development perspective and a traditional business economic perspective.

Simultaneously, it is extremely important to root or embed your sustainability identity and your sustainability measures and initiatives within the local environment, the local community and the social network(s) your hospitality company is a part of. This is where the consequences of your actions are felt the most. This is the context that influences the decisions and behaviour of both your customers and staff. These are the stakeholders whose support you require to ensure your long-term social licence to operate. This is where you can tap into, and join forces with, the so-called grassroots movements that are likely to play a crucial role in transforming our socio-economic system into one that is truly based on principles such as inclusiveness, equality and a responsible way of interacting with our natural environment.

Sustainable business models

Obviously, accounting for all of these reference points would impact the way you operate as a company. You would interact differently with your environment than most (other) companies do. Fully integrating sustainability principles into the core business strategy, tactics and operations of your company would influence all decisions you make and all actions you take. In other words, this would fundamentally change the rationale of your business model. *Traditionally*, a company's business model is defined as describing the rationale of how a company creates value, delivers value and captures value (Osterwalder and Pigneur, 2010). It relates to (1) the products/services/experiences you offer or provide to customers, as well as the way you produce these products/services/experiences and the natural resources needed for producing them, (2) the way in which you then deliver these products/services/experiences to your customers, and (3) the way in which you deal with costs and revenues (Bocken *et al.*, 2014).

Hospitality businesses and professionals are far from the only ones that could contribute to achieving sustainable development. In fact, over the years, numerous (other types of) companies have already adjusted their business models in order to improve their sustainability performance. You could distinguish at least three levels or generations of sustainable business models applied by companies, based on the way they have actually integrated sustainability principles into their core business strategy, tactics and operations (Melissen and Moratis, 2016):

1. The first level or generation relates to companies that have focused on redesigning their products and services, and applying recycling, cradle-to-cradle and circular economy principles in trying to minimise or avoid pollution and in trying to maximise material, water and energy efficiency of their products/services/experiences and the way they produce them. Some of these companies also apply leasing instead of selling their products, and some use renewable energy sources. What characterises this first generation of sustainable business models is that companies that apply them mainly focus on reducing their negative environmental impact. This may come across as a rather narrow perspective on sustainable development but, to be fair, some companies have really managed to drastically change the way they operate. For instance, some of them have

been able to significantly reduce their ecological footprint, or have even managed to turn their day-to-day operations into being carbon neutral. Others have managed to redesign their products in such a way that they no longer require materials or substances that are scarce, that need to be flown in from across our globe or that involve cutting down rainforests or disturbing vulnerable ecosystems to acquire them.

2. The second level or generation relates to companies that not only account for their environmental impacts but also for their social and economic impacts. These days, a number of companies, especially size-able and internationally operating companies listed on stock exchanges, actually (voluntarily) report on how they have managed to *balance* the well-known three Ps of sustainable development; people, planet, profit. Many of these companies publicly *acknowledge* that making money is not, and cannot, be their only responsibility. Therefore, they focus on generating profits in a way that minimises the burden on our natural environment and people. Besides trying to minimise the environmental damages linked to (producing and delivering) their products/services/experiences, some of these companies also invest in the health and well-being of their employees, whereas others choose to get involved with improving living conditions in local communities or charity projects aimed at improving ecosystems or economies across the world.

3. The third level or generation relates to so-called social or societal business models. These business models are based on the rationale of creating economic value through creating societal value (Porter and Kramer, 2011). Ultimately, the premise of these business models is to treat profitability as a means to an end – for instance, solving specific environmental problems or community development, not an end in itself (Wilson and Post, 2013). In other words, these businesses aim at solving specific sustainability problems but have made the choice to do so through operating as a business on the free market and not as, for instance, a non-governmental agency relying on donations for funding its operations.

Unfortunately, despite the possible good intentions of those making decisions in many of the companies applying any of these three generations of sustainable business models, it would be fair to say that the business world's contribution to achieving sustainable development has, so far, been rather limited. Numerous companies have engaged in a range of well-meant sustainability measures and initiatives, but these have not fundamentally changed our socio-economic system and, thus, do not contribute to *actually* escaping the lock-in described in the previous chapter. To put it simply, these companies, even those applying societal business models, still operate within the confines of our current socio-economic system. Some of them may have found less unsustainable ways of producing their products or less unsustainable ways of delivering them to their customers, but the third key element of their business models has not really changed. They still rely on making profit for long-term survival. In fact, by purposely living by the *rules* of the free market, they still rely on capturing (as much) value (as possible) from that market to survive. In other words, they still focus on money, and exchange of money for products and services, as the overriding principle guiding their actions. These actions are still very much aimed at trying to increase market share in order to increase profits and be able to satisfy shareholders and banks, whose support is needed to acquire the materials and financial resources to *scale up* and to be able to produce and deliver those products efficiently, and thus be able to sell them to customers for a price they are willing to pay. Consequently, many of the companies applying first and second generation sustainable business models are increasingly 'looking for ways to engage in corporate social responsibility that simultaneously improves their economic performance, thus increasingly treating environmental and social practices as a business case' (Melissen and Moratis, 2016). They continue to engage in sustainability initiatives, but these are increasingly judged on their contribution to business economic criteria such as cost reductions, risk reduction and profit margins (Schaltegger *et al.*, 2011). As Marques and Mintzberg (2015) put it, sustainability measures and initiatives are usually treated as add-ons – as the icing on the cake.

For those companies applying third generation sustainable business models, the situation is actually not that different, even though their mission statements oftentimes explicitly claim profit margins are not what drive them and that they are *in it* for different reasons. They still need to make a profit to survive. They still need to satisfy demands from those funding them. They are still in competition with other companies for the customers' money. By choosing to operate as a company on the free market, they still need to meet many of the same requirements as those operating on the same free market without the *burden* of simultaneously trying to create societal value. This explains why many of these *societal businesses* have not managed to move beyond being a niche player in the overall game being played. Unfortunately, by choosing to play the existing game based on the existing rules, these businesses and professionals have not been able to fundamentally change (the role of the business world in) our socio-economic system and, thus, have also not (yet) assisted us in escaping the lock-in of this system. As a consequence, actual progress with respect to achieving sustainable development of our societies is still not nearly enough to avoid the predictions of the Club of Rome, as discussed in Chapter 1, coming true.

Therefore, if businesses and professionals truly want to make a significant contribution to avoiding these consequences, and to adjusting the course of our societies to a sustainable one, they need to apply sustainable business models that move beyond these first three levels or generations. They need to apply business models that help us escape the lock-in of our current socio-economic system, and that assist us in developing an alternative system that is based on the principles of sustainable development. Obviously, this means that those business models are based on *not* treating sustainability as an add-on, *not* focusing on values such as private property, autonomy and economic growth, and *not* relying on Adam Smith's (1776) claim that focusing on self-interest is in our common interest (see Chapter 3). As Lüdeke-Freund explains (2009, pp. 66–67), these businesses and professionals need to create a business model that is based on an 'activity system of a firm which allocates resources and coordinates activities in a value creation process which overcomes the public/private benefit discrepancy' by 'extending value propositions to integrate public and private benefits [. . .], making customers involved and responsible partners in value creation processes [. . .], taking advantage of partnerships which enhance resources and activities [. . .], [. . .] and dedicating resources and activities to [. . .] explore currently neglected opportunities in non-market spheres' (Lüdeke-Freund, 2009, pp. 66–67).

In other words, these business models, which we could refer to as fourth generation sustainable business models, need to be based on aligning the interests of the company with the interests of wider society (Melissen and Moratis, 2016; Smit and Melissen, 2018). Doing so involves developing the new social technologies discussed in the previous chapter. As has been established in Chapter 5, developing these new social technologies can only be done in collaboration with relevant stakeholders and will probably mostly rely on bottom-up innovation taking place in local communities and social networks. A company that wants to join forces with these communities and networks will need to be able to convey to their members that they 'have got what it takes to be part of a community or network that is based on long-term commitment and true reciprocity rather than short-term gains and opportunism' (Melissen and Moratis, 2016, p.15). This involves developing the type of relationships with the members of these communities and networks that make them trust you, as a company, but that also involve giving up some autonomy and sharing power when it comes to decisions with respect to what specific *needs* this community or network sets out to satisfy, and in what way (Loorbach, 2014; Stubbs and Cocklin, 2008). Obviously, this involves all of the things discussed in Chapter 4, such as communicating openly and honestly about your intentions, backing these up with the decisions you make and the actions you take, and, thus, creating and living up to a coherent and transparent (sustainability) identity that complements the identity of the community or network. And, finally, as a company, you obviously need the support of your customers in all this. As a company, you can only make a significant and *sustained* contribution to achieving sustainable development if your own customers are on board; if they are willing to buy and consume your sustainable products/services/experiences and assist you in making your sustainability measures and initiatives a success.

In summary, a fourth generation sustainable business model is based on incorporating the following types of mechanisms (Melissen and Moratis, 2016):

1. Mechanisms that allow the company to account for the complexities of human behaviour in relation to promoting sustainable decisions and behaviour by their customers.
2. Mechanisms that allow the company to create a coherent and transparent sustainability identity.
3. Mechanisms that allow the company to join forces with local communities and social networks in bottom-up innovation aimed at developing the new social technologies needed for viable alternatives to our current socio-economic system.

CASE 6.1

New hotel policy in Amsterdam – QO Amsterdam

Introduction

Amsterdam is one of those cities that suffers from overtourism. Consequently, it would be fair to say that we are nearing the limit when it comes the hotel market in the city of Amsterdam. The municipality of Amsterdam has therefore initiated a policy that it will not allow new hotels in big parts of the city. In some areas of Amsterdam, hotels could be built, but only if, simply put, they can show they would contribute to innovation, improving the local community, sustainability and social entrepreneurship.

One of the initiatives for a new hotel that has managed to meet those requirements is the one for QO Amsterdam (QO hereafter), part of the Intercontinental Hotel Group. The hotel, where a luxurious stay is combined with sustainability, opened in April 2018. The hotel features 288 rooms, 21 floors, one restaurant and a bar, a wellness studio and a rooftop greenhouse.

What do they do?

Every aspect of QO is designed to have a positive impact on the world and to ensure the most pleasant experience for guests. Guests are defined as travellers *and* the local community. The hotel features technological innovations such as a living building, which means that moving panels react to the outdoor weather conditions and ensure comfort in the guest rooms by providing insulation or allowing natural sunlight to heat the rooms. Floor to ceiling windows take care of light provision during the day, limiting the need for electrical lighting. QO also thought of little things, such as a paper strap around a pair of slippers rather than a plastic wrapping. Menus in its restaurant are based on products from the rooftop greenhouse. The greenhouse even has its own Facebook page with updates on what is being produced and for what purpose. On their website they display clips of staff – mostly executive staff – telling the story of QO and what sustainability means for them.

According to this story, the hotel is not just packed with state-of-the-art technology; it also wants to play an important role in the local community. It claims to also work together with the local community and to serve as a gathering place for like-minded people.

Figure 6.1 The rooftop greenhouse at QO Amsterdam
Courtesy of: QO

So what?

As the General Manager of the hotel commented in the press: 'A compromise between luxury and sustainable should not be necessary, we would like to show that those two can go hand in hand'.

We, the authors of this book, would argue that QO is certainly trying to move beyond applying a typical second level or generation sustainable business model. Sustainability is definitely *not* treated as an add-on; it is a crucial element of the business model applied by this particular hotel. What is more, the people involved with setting up the hotel obviously managed to convince the Amsterdam authorities that they are contributing to innovation, improving the local community, sustainability and social entrepreneurship.

And yes, some of the technologies applied in this hotel represent state-of-the-art ways of minimising your carbon footprint. The hotel clearly focuses on local produce in their menus. It even uses urban farming to produce its own ingredients. And, obviously, local residents can visit the restaurant and bar of the hotel. In fact, the wellness studio is also accessible for local residents.

Is this enough to qualify as a third or fourth generation sustainable business model? Is this the type of experimenting we need to create a sustainable alternative to our current socio-economic system? Will this establishment be able to avoid some of the pitfalls involved with being part of an international chain? Time will tell. We, the authors of this book, will certainly look out for updates and third-party reports on their efforts *and results* with great interest, as we do with respect to many of the other cases and examples included in this book, as well as some of the other interesting new developments and initiatives *out there*. We encourage you, our reader, to do the same.

Source: Gemeente Amsterdam, www.amsterdam.nl

QO Amsterdam, www.qo-amsterdam.nl

Sustainable hospitality business models

Obviously, the key question within the context of this book is: what *level* or *generation* of sustainable business model could, and should, hospitality companies apply? Simply put, these days, the first level really is a must. Within today's market place, it will be almost impossible to survive, as a company, if you do not at least address and try to minimise your own negative environmental impact. Governments might be slow in reacting to the signals that warn us about the detrimental consequences of continuing on our unsustainable path as a society, but slowly but surely legislation is starting to put some requirements in place with respect to companies' environmental impacts. We, the customers buying and consuming hospitality experiences, might still be inclined to often favour our short-term personal interests over the long-term common good in deciding on which experiences we want, but, simultaneously, more and more of us are quite worried about what is happening to our world and do feel that the business world, including the hospitality industry, has an important role to play in addressing this problem.

What is more, we increasingly pay attention to what the media and our peers say, for instance, through what they report on online review sites, about the sustainability initiatives and measures of hospitality companies. More and more of us are quite conscious about what we eat and drink, and a growing number of us prefer local, seasonal, organic and even vegetarian or vegan options. This trend is especially relevant for hospitality companies, given that providing food and drink is an integral part of most hospitality experiences. If hospitality companies are in the news for blatantly ignoring their environmental impact, like with any other type of company, we are inclined to hold a grudge, and we will likely think twice before buying what those companies have to offer us. What is more, an important part of the customer base of specific types of hospitality companies, such as hotels, consists of business clients. Business guests often form half or even more of the total customer base. Many of these business clients will not buy from a hospitality company if it cannot prove, for instance, through dedicated labels or certifications, that it at least adheres to certain minimum requirements or standards with respect to addressing its environmental impact. Together, these developments imply that applying at least the first level or generation of sustainable business model has now become the norm. Not living up to this norm would seriously undermine the social licence to operate *and* the (medium- to long-term) business economic performance of a hospitality company.

In fact, for most, if not all, hospitality companies the same could be said for second level or generation sustainable business models. As Chapter 4 has shown, also addressing the social component of sustainable development and treating your employees well and involving them in defining and shaping your sustainability measures and initiatives are both the right and the smart things to do, in every sense. As Chapter 5 has shown, especially for hospitality companies, it is also crucial to account for the interests of local residents and businesses. These residents and businesses oftentimes form an integral part of the overall hospitality experience of customers. Obviously, as Smit and Melissen (2018, p. 232) explain, you cannot expect these residents and businesses to 'welcome your guests or visitors with open arms' if your hotel or restaurant has caused local bed and breakfasts and lunch rooms to go out of business or 'if your festival, conference or theme park disturbs the local community through causing traffic jams or noise [and] pollution'. What is more, for hospitality companies of a certain size, for instance internationally operating hotel and restaurant chains, reporting on their environmental *and* social impact is a must. Shareholders, banks, licensing parties, the media and a number of other stakeholders simply will not accept anything less than Triple Bottom Line reporting (Elkington, 1997) and a clear vision and plan with respect to the company's Corporate Social Responsibility or Corporate Citizenship. Therefore, regardless of whether your particular hospitality establishment is an independent local company or part of a bigger whole, such as an internationally operating chain, once again, a choice to not at least apply a second level or generation sustainable business model is likely to undermine your social licence to operate *and* your (medium- to long-term) business economic performance. Consequently, it would be fair to say that acknowledging and addressing your environmental *and* social impact really is something all hospitality companies could *and* should do. There are numerous different ways in which you could do this – some of which have been discussed in this book and a wealth of additional guidelines, tips, tricks and best practices are widely available – and many of those do not involve huge investments but rather a choice. There really is no excuse and, to be blunt, it would be rather senseless for hospitality businesses and professionals to consciously make unsustainable choices and not, at the very least, apply a business model that accounts for all of the company's direct sustainability impacts.

However, the hospitality industry's contribution to achieving sustainable development of our societies need not stop there. Earlier, some of the complications of applying a third level or generation sustainable business model have been highlighted. It would be fair to say that quite a few of the companies that apply this type of business model have found it rather difficult to walk the fine line between focusing on creating societal value and still meeting the demands of operating in the free market as a company (Santos *et al.*, 2015). In practice, many of these companies have found it difficult to scale up or have had to make concessions to their original mission and ambitions to survive (Melissen and Moratis, 2016). Simultaneously, this type of company is invaluable from a sustainable development perspective. If the business world is going to make a truly significant contribution to tackling our biggest societal challenge, it simply must find ways to move beyond treating sustainability measures and initiatives as add-ons and business cases – from a *traditional* business economic perspective – and it needs to explore (how to take on) a new role in how we, as humanity, have arranged our world to satisfy our needs. A sustainable alternative to our current socio-economic system cannot be based on one of the key players in that system sticking to the rules and principles of the *old* system. Based on everything discussed so far, one could argue that if any industry could give applying and experimenting with societal business models a good try, it would be the hospitality industry. The companies in this industry represent natural stakeholders in social, environmental and economic systems at all levels of the 'global-local nexus' (Saarinen, 2006, p. 1134) of our biggest societal challenge. These companies are very much intertwined with local and regional social, environmental and economic systems, and they could not only contribute significantly to achieving sustainable development of these systems, but they also represent key beneficiaries of developing them in a sustainable direction. The valuation of their core product by their customers is reliant on these local and regional systems; they increasingly form an integral part of the overall experience of their customers. Finally, that same core product is designed to make people feel happy, to install fond memories, to show them a good time. Therefore, if you would have to pick any type of company to have the motivation and the appropriate expertise, skills and attitude – together oftentimes referred to as competencies – to step up to the plate, it would be a hospitality company.

The Eden Project, which was highlighted in the previous chapter, represents a very nice example of a hospitality company that could be argued to already apply a societal business model, and an example of a company that has already showed that it can actually work. This is far from the only example already *out there* though. In their book on sustainable customer experience design, Smit and Melissen (2018) mention quite a few more examples. For instance, in the events sector of the hospitality industry, we can witness a significant increase in events that are purposely staged for promoting sustainable products, services and behaviour, and quite a few of them have proven to be successful, also from a business economic perspective. More and more restaurants, lunchrooms and other types of businesses in the food and drinks sector of the hospitality industry have explicitly been established to promote sustainable food and drinks, or to create jobs for people with a so-called distance to the labour market and to show others that they need not and should not be overlooked. With respect to the latter, it is important to note, once again, that, contrary to what some people think, achieving sustainable development of our societies is not just about reducing CO_2 emissions and saving our natural environment. It is also very much about 'social inclusion, social justice and greater equity [. . .] precisely because without it we will not solve the environmental problems' (Washington, 2015, p. 107) we face. If any industry could, and really should, take the lead in this regard, it would be an industry that is all about interactions between people and focusing on the needs, values, priorities and preferences of individuals; the hospitality industry.

For exactly the same reasons that hospitality businesses and professionals need not and should not limit themselves to applying first and second generation sustainable business models, and could be the ones showing us that societal business models can be applied successfully, one could also argue that if any type of company could set out to fully align its interests with the interests of wider society, it would be a hospitality company. The previous subsection concluded with highlighting three mechanisms that need to be incorporated in a business model to be able to turn that business model into a fourth level or generation sustainable business model. By now, surely, you will have noticed that these three types of mechanisms correspond with the topics of the previous chapters of this book. We, the authors of this book, could claim that this is a coincidence but . . . obviously, it is not.

The introduction of this book has already stated that we have purposely set out to describe *what could be* instead of *what is*. Based on the train of thought presented so far, we hope that you will agree with us that there is every reason to not accept the current state of sustainability in the hospitality industry. Why would this industry, as is often claimed, have to lag behind other industries and sectors when it comes to its contribution to achieving sustainable development of our societies? The previous chapters have shown that the opportunities to turn this situation around are there. Some of the roads for aligning the interests of a hospitality company with the common good might prove difficult ones and require some effort, but they are all but closed down. In fact, we would argue that the opposite is true. Given all that has been discussed so far, it actually makes no sense for this industry to stick to treating sustainability as an add-on to business as usual. It is perfectly positioned to move well beyond such a limited approach to sustainability measures and initiatives. It is also in the long-term best interest of hospitality businesses and professionals themselves to no longer assume that hospitality and sustainability represent two mutually exclusive concepts. Like any other type of business, hospitality companies' social licence to operate and business economic outlook will deteriorate rapidly in years to come, if they do not find a way to adjust their core product in a sustainable direction. Ignoring the increasing relevance and urgency of the biggest societal challenge of our times is the real dead end. This is especially true for companies that rely so heavily on their direct surroundings, the natural and social (eco)systems they are located in and closely connected to, for how their customers will value their offer to them. How can you make your customers feel welcome and install fond memories in a *hostile* environment? How can you continue to serve them food and drinks, as an integral part of the experience you stage for them, if our food production system is one of the first to come under pressure as a result of an unsustainable way of arranging our world to satisfy our needs? How can you focus on hospitality as your unique selling point in a world that no longer represents a hospitable environment for humanity?

Hospitality and sustainability need not be mutually exclusive concepts; their true core principles are actually the same. Sustainable development is all about meeting people's needs, accounting for their values, preferences and priorities, and finding ways to interact with each other based on inclusiveness, equality and a sustainable relationship with our natural world. Ultimately, the essence of hospitality represents a crucial concept for achieving sustainable development. Therefore, to put it bluntly and without meaning to offend those who already dedicate their time and energy to doing so, it is about time that the industry of the same name stops *wallowing* in ignorance and refusing to step out of its *role* as the villain with no other choice and, instead, starts to live up to its potential to serve as a catalyst for achieving sustainable development of our societies.

So, there we have it: a clear *call for action*, as promised in the introduction of this book. Hospitality businesses and professionals are in the perfect position to experiment with and apply third and fourth level or generation sustainable business models. They are the ones that could step up to plate when it comes to creating a new role for the business world in our societies and creating sustainable alternatives to our current socio-economic system. These businesses and professionals could play a key role in promoting sustainable behaviour well beyond the *formal* boundaries of the hospitality industry, finding ways to sidestep social dilemmas and avoiding humanity's tragedy of the commons, and developing the physical and, especially, the social technologies needed for doing so, acting as a key member of grass-roots movements and as a bottom-up co-innovator and co-creator. What is more, doing so is not only the *right* thing to do, from a sustainable development perspective, but also the *smart* thing to do, in *every* sense of the word.

Competencies for sustainability

The obvious follow-up question to this call for action is: what are the details of these physical and social technologies, and of the resulting business processes and models, that these hospitality businesses and professionals need to develop, install and apply? This is where things get *a bit complicated*.

Obviously, the authors of this book are not the only ones calling for action with respect to the business world's contribution to achieving sustainable development of our societies. They are far from the first and only ones to realise that the business world is 'inextricably both part of the problem as well as the solution' (Warhurst, 2005, p. 155). Consequently, numerous researchers, professionals, activists, policy-makers and others have already put in quite some time and effort in trying to formulate, shape and experiment with the details of these technologies, processes and models. Unfortunately, *we* have not found *the* answer to all questions yet. We have not yet been able to figure out all relevant details of all the required physical and social technologies, value creation processes and resulting business models for all relevant contexts. This is hardly surprising because if it were that simple, we would have managed to adjust the course of our societies already. If changing the way we have arranged our world to satisfy our needs was that easy, we would probably not find ourselves in the pickle we are in.

Simultaneously, given the gravity of the situation, we simply cannot afford to wait with making changes until we have found *the* answer and figured out all details. We cannot wait for our governments and policy-makers to (finally) realise that we *do* need progressive sustainability regulations and dramatic revisions of our tax systems. Even though customers' preferences and behaviours are slowly but surely moving in a more sustainable direction, the invisible hand of the free market will not suddenly make all companies shout out *Eureka!*, have a collective light bulb moment and instantaneously adjust all of their products, services and production and delivery processes to exactly those ones that we need to avoid all negative consequences of our behaviour, as humanity, thus far, and repair the damages already done.

Therefore, what is needed is for as many people and organisations as possible to step up to the plate and make changes, right here and right now, based on what we *do* know and what we *can* do. And, luckily, we actually already know a lot, and we can already do a lot. For instance, over the course of the last few decades, scientific research has pointed out and helped us understand many of the interactions between local, regional and global environmental, social and economic systems that we need to account for in creating a sustainable alternative to our current socio-economic system. Researchers and the business world have developed numerous physical technologies that could assist us in repairing some of the damages already done and avoiding future problems. Grassroots movements and local communities are already experimenting with interesting new social technologies that could play a crucial role in pursuing inclusiveness, equality and a sustainable relationship with our natural environment.

Your role as a hospitality professional

This is where you, the reader of this book, come in. Given that you were probably stimulated by your professor, your boss or your colleagues to read it – or maybe it was your own choice based on reading a review or a summary of the contents on a website or social media, we, the authors, assume that you are either a current or a future hospitality professional, or a current or future professional in a related field. Based on all that has been discussed so far, we hope that you now realise that this puts you in a *special* position that comes with a *special* responsibility. This book has argued that the hospitality industry is perfectly positioned to act as a catalyst for achieving sustainable development of our societies. It has also discussed particular avenues for doing so. Simultaneously, it has pointed out that this industry, as a whole, is currently not (yet) realising this potential. And, finally, it has shown that this status quo need not be a given but rather represents a choice and, to make a long story short, the *wrong* choice, in every sense of the word.

Therefore, it is now up to you to turn things around. You are the one who will have to look into possibilities to apply new physical and social technologies in the particular hospitality company in which you (will) work. Together with your (future) colleagues, you will need to figure out how to adjust the value creation processes and business model of your company in a sustainable direction. Together with your customers and other relevant stakeholders, especially those in your local community and social networks, you will need to convey, discuss and deliver on what role your company could play in satisfying their needs, and in co-creating sustainable ways of doing so.

Obviously, the details of the particular sustainable technologies, processes, business model and role of your particular company depend upon your particular context. What type of company are you/will you be working for? Is it a small independent hospitality business or is it a local establishment of a big internationally operating chain? Are you/will you be working in one of those local establishments or at headquarters? Have you started/ will you start your own company? What is the core product of your company? What do the direct natural surroundings and local community in which you are located look like, and what are the most pressing sustainability problems for this particular context?

Obviously, the specific physical technologies that could assist you in sustainably transporting visitors to your theme park are very different technologies than those needed to sustainably heat or cool your restaurant. Then again, both are still based on replacing non-renewable energy sources with renewable ones. The social technologies needed to play a role in achieving sustainable development of your local community, if your down-to-earth and very reasonably priced bed and breakfast is located in an impoverished part of town, are likely to not be exactly the same as those needed to play a role in achieving sustainable development of the local community, if your theatre focusing on modern dance performances is located in the richest part of town, where income is not the main problem but rather poor air quality is. Once again though, in both instances you will need to communicate openly and honestly about your intentions and gain the trust of local stakeholders to have them join forces with you. Guests of the bed and breakfast might be very different *types* of people than those attending performances in the theatre, but both groups of customers are still people. For both groups, you will need to account for their values, preferences and priorities if you want to involve them in your sustainability measures and initiatives.

Therefore, as Smit and Melissen (2018, p. 219) explain, 'even though the details of sustainable [technologies, processes and] business models might differ depending on the context in which they are applied, the basic reference points on which they are based will be the same' and 'the train of thought that you will have to apply [...] will be quite similar'. Even more so for companies that all belong to one and the same industry and thus, ultimately, offer the same type of final product to their customers: hospitality experiences. Regardless of whether you are/will be working in a fancy restaurant or a hip and trendy lunchroom, a five star traditional conference hotel or a theme park with thrilling rollercoaster rides, a high-brow theatre or a community centre that hosts AA meetings and mindfulness sessions for unemployed youngsters from broken homes, applying sustainable hospitality business models must be based on successfully combining hospitality principles and sustainability principles. Fundamentally, these principles do not change; you just need to apply them in concert with each other, and in a way that matches the particular context in which you do so.

Sustainable hospitality competencies

Therefore, if you want to contribute to improving sustainability in the hospitality industry, you need specific competencies – expertise, skills and attitude – to successfully face the teasing paradox referred to in Chapter 1. Sustainable development is increasingly becoming a topic that deserves the attention of the hospitality industry, and it is now obvious that this industry could actually play a vital role in tackling this urgent societal challenge. Meanwhile, many of its core products and business models are still based on contrasting values, such as oversupplying customers, only linking to their hedonic motives, unsustainable ways of staging these hospitality experiences, and ignoring the interests of other relevant stakeholders, the local community and the natural environment.

Obviously, successfully facing this paradox is all about adjusting these core products and business models in such a way that they could contribute to achieving sustainable development of our societies, while still being able to convince (enough) customers to buy and consume them. A hospitality company still needs customers to survive, and to be able to play its role in adjusting the way we have arranged our world to satisfy our needs. Therefore, a sustainable hospitality company still stages hospitality experiences for its customers. However, the experiences it stages, and the way in which it does so, will probably be somewhat different from *traditional* hospitality experiences and *traditional* (*service-with-a-smile* and *the-customer-is-king*) ways of staging them. What is more, the company's vision and mission, as well as its identity, that support the design, staging and management of these experiences are likely to be based on values that move beyond merely *making money*.

Consequently, sustainable hospitality competencies are also a bit different from *traditional* hospitality competencies. These traditional hospitality competencies tend to focus on how to create value through staging hospitality experiences based on understanding the needs and wishes of customers, creating a welcoming atmosphere, cultural sensitivity, designing, managing and (continuously) improving so-called on-stage and back-stage processes, accounting for legal and financial aspects, and so on (cf. Lub *et al.*, 2018). Many of these aspects are also important for creating a sustainable hospitality company. Therefore, these aspects also constitute important ingredients for sustainable hospitality competencies.

However, if you are to make a significant contribution to improving sustainability in the hospitality industry, you cannot focus solely on monetary value; you also need to focus on societal value, maybe even more so than monetary value. You also cannot focus only on creating a welcoming atmosphere within the confines of your establishment; you also need to focus on the surroundings, the local community and the natural environment. In fact, an important part of fulfilling your role in achieving sustainable development of your local community could very well be to apply your expertise on creating a welcoming atmosphere, to ensuring that sustainability initiatives in your local community 'and resulting benefits reach all inhabitants of the local community, not just those eager and confident enough to step in at the early stages' (Melissen, 2016, p. 26). Cultural sensitivity is not limited to understanding the values, preferences and priorities of your customers in order to please them, but it is also vital for convincing them to support and join you in making your sustainability measures and initiatives a success. In fact, you also want to use this understanding as the foundation for promoting sustainable decisions and behaviour by your customers once they have left your premises and have returned to their daily lives. Obviously, you can use this same knowledge and expertise with respect to what makes people tick in building the relationships and trust needed for jointly engaging in experiments with sustainable alternatives to our current socio-economic system with local stakeholders and members of your social networks. Sometimes, these experiments might involve creating opportunities and room for *not* sticking to the rules of the *old* game. In other words, instead of accounting for legal and financial aspects through following the guidelines of our current socio-economic system, creating a truly sustainable business model for your hospitality company might very well involve 'lobbying and teaming up with influential others to persuade policy makers and public authorities to adjust regulatory systems or to at least allow you [and your co-experimenters] to not follow current regulations to the letter' (Melissen, 2016, p. 22).

Maybe the best way to highlight these additions or updates to traditional hospitality competencies is to refer to them as applying a specific way of reasoning in handling all of these aspects. Melissen and Moratis (2016, 2017) have labelled this way of reasoning as sustainability intelligence, and they have distinguished three distinct types of sustainability intelligence to constitute the key reference points for creating and applying sustainable business models:

1. Naïve intelligence
2. Native intelligence
3. Narrative intelligence

The first relates to the need to look at things differently, and to having the freshness, openness and intuitiveness to come up and experiment with viable alternatives to our current socio-economic system. It also relates to perseverance and not getting discouraged or frustrated by possible raised eyebrows from those who find it difficult to escape the lock-in of our current system in thinking of ways to arrange our world to satisfy our needs. In other words, this type of intelligence links to the courage and doggedness that is needed to focus on doing things in ways that might very well be labelled naïve by others.

Native intelligence refers to understanding people and how they could be persuaded and motivated to make sustainable decisions, and to engage in sustainable behaviour. It links to everything that has been discussed in Chapter 3, including avenues for tapping into the evolutionary processes that explain many of our decisions and behaviours, even today. This type of intelligence links to resolving potential conflicts between hedonic, gain and normative goals, nudging us, influencing us through creating specific contexts, and using the tendencies in our Stone Age brains for promoting sustainability, convincing others of (the relevance of) your sustainability measures and initiatives and allowing you to support and join theirs.

Finally, narrative intelligence refers to making full use of the fact that we, humans, are *narrative animals* (Mateas & Sengers, 1999). If you want your customers to buy and consume your sustainable hospitality experiences, and support and join you in making your sustainability measures and initiatives a success, they need to understand the logic and benefits of doing so. If you want to join forces with other (local) stakeholders in achieving sustainable development of your local community or natural environment, you need to co-create a clear description of what it is you will be doing, and how. You need a story, an appealing picture, and you need to be able to convey what you will be bringing to the table. Therefore, open and honest communication and storytelling techniques are crucial to making all of this work.

In summary, sustainable hospitality competencies – the expertise, skills and attitude needed to create and apply sustainable hospitality business models and to convince others to support and join you in making them a success – could be argued to represent an updated version of traditional hospitality competencies. They constitute a future-proof version of the good old hospitality competencies, by injecting them with sustainability intelligence, so to speak. Your challenge, as a current or future hospitality professional, is to apply them wisely. Maybe you (will) work in one of those big international restaurant or hotel chains. Then, you could use the train of thought presented in this book, and all of the ingredients of these competencies, to convince your colleagues or your bosses to allow you to set up a new division or a new establishment to explore where your core product could take you in terms of making a contribution to achieving sustainable development of our societies. Maybe you (will) work in a small independent company and you could use this book as inspiration to join forces with other businesses and local residents in making your local community a better place to live in, in every sense of the word and for all people involved. The simple fact is that we, the authors, cannot tell you what to do and how to use the reference points discussed in this book. We do not know all details of the particular circumstances of your professional and personal life. We cannot account for all possible complications that you might have to deal with, be it a management contract with little wiggle room or limited financial resources. Then again, it is crystal clear that it is about time that more hospitality professionals step up to the plate, make a conscious choice to no longer focus on *what is*, and to focus on co-creating *what could be* and *what should be*, together with all of those engaged citizens, entrepreneurs, professionals, civil servants, researchers and activists already *out there*. We can only hope that you will be one of them.

SUMMARY

Based on reading this chapter, we hope you will understand and remember the following:

- Pursuing sustainable development need not be complicated.
- Sustainable development is not as much about technology as it is about people.
- Fully integrating, deciding and acting on sustainability principles requires the support of a number of stakeholders:
  - customers;
  - staff;
  - local environment/community and social network.
- Why traditional business models need to be transformed into sustainable business models.
- The first three levels or generations of sustainable business models.
- Why it is important to move beyond these first three levels and move to a fourth generation sustainable business model.
- The mechanisms to be incorporated in fourth generation sustainable business models.
- Hospitality business should, at the very least, apply second generation sustainable business models but they very well could apply third and fourth generation sustainable business models.
- Why hospitality companies can successfully align interests of the wider society with their own interests, and thus should not lag behind other types of companies.
- Ignoring the relevance and urgency of achieving sustainable development is the real dead end.
- Focusing on sustainability is not only the right thing to do, but also the smart thing to do.

- (Future) hospitality professionals have a special position with a special responsibility.
- The logic of sustainable hospitality competencies.
- The three types of sustainability intelligence needed to create and apply truly sustainable hospitality business models.

FOOD FOR THOUGHT

Based on the content of this chapter, the following questions, challenges and topics could serve as interesting starting points for further discussion:

- Choose three different hospitality businesses and establish which level of sustainable business model they are currently applying.
- What other elements of sustainable hospitality competencies could you think of?
- How do you see your role, as a (future) hospitality professional, in relation to achieving sustainable development?

References

Bocken, N., Short, S., Rana, P. & Evans, S. (2014). 'A literature and practice review to develop sustainable business model archetypes'. *Journal of Cleaner Production*, 65, 42–56.

Elkington, J. (1997). *Cannibals with forks: the triple bottom line of 21st century business*. Oxford: Capstone.

Lub, X., Breuker, H. & Tomaszewski, L. (2018). 'Competencies and leadership'. In F. Melissen, J.P. van de Rest, S. Josephi & R. Blomme (eds.) *Hospitality Experience* (second edition) (pp. 251–270). Groningen: Noordhoff Uitgevers.

Lüdeke-Freund, F. (2009). *Business model concepts in corporate sustainability contexts: from rhetoric to a generic template for 'business models for sustainability'*. *Working paper*. Lüneberg: Center for Sustainability Management, Leuphana Universität Lüneburg.

Marques, J. & Mintzberg, H. (2015). 'Why corporate social responsibility isn't a piece of cake'. *MIT Sloan Management Review*, 56, 7–11.

Mateas, M. & Sengers, P. (1999). Narrative intelligence. *Proceedings of the AAAI fall symposium on narrative intelligence* (pp. 1–10). Palo Alto, CA: AAAI Press.

Melissen, F. (2016). *Fourth generation sustainable business models* (inaugural speech). Breda: NHTV Breda University of Applied Sciences.

Melissen, F. & Moratis, L. (2016). 'A call for fourth generation sustainable business models'. *The Journal of Corporate Citizenship*, 63, 8–16.

Melissen, F. & Moratis, L. (2017). 'Developing fourth generation sustainability-oriented business models: towards naïve, native, and narrative intelligence'. In S.O. Idowu, S. Vertigans & A. Schiopoiu Burlea (eds.) *Corporate social responsibility in times of crisis: practices and cases from Europe, Africa and the world* (pp. 59–76). Berlin: Springer.

Osterwalder, A. & Pigneur, Y. (2010). *Business model generation: A handbook for visionaries, game changers, and challengers*. Hoboken: John Wiley & Sons.

Porter, M. & Kramer, M. (2011). 'Creating shared value'. *Harvard Business Review*, 89, 62–77.

Saarinen, J. (2006). 'Traditions of sustainability in tourism studies'. *Annals of Tourism Research*, 33(4),1121–1140.

Santos, F., Pache, A.-C. & Birkholz, C. (2015). 'Making hybrids work: aligning business models and organizational design for social enterprises. *California Management Review*, 57, 36–58.

Schaltegger, S., Lüdeke-Freund, F. & Hansen, E. (2011). *Business cases for sustainability and the role of business model innovation: developing a conceptual framework*. Lüneberg: Centre for Sustainability Management.

Smit, B. & Melissen, F. (2018). *Sustainable customer experience design: co-creating experiences in events, tourism and hospitality*. New York: Routledge.

Stubbs, W. & Cocklin, C. (2008). 'Conceptualizing a "sustainable business model"'. *Organization & Environment*, 21(2),103–127.

Warhurst, A. (2005). 'Future roles of business in society: the expanding boundaries of corporate social responsibility and a compelling case for partnership'. *Futures*, 37(2), 151–168.

Washington, H. (2015). *Demystifying sustainability: towards real solutions*. London: Routledge.

Wilson, F. & Post, J. (2013). 'Business model for people, planet (& profits): exploring the phenomena of social business, a market-based approach to social value creation'. *Small Business Economics*, 40(3), 715–737.

Index

Manufactured by Amazon.ca
Bolton, ON

24230570R00081